GW01003562

Ta[ble of Contents]

Part I.   Basic Use Cases

Foreword

I have many tools in my web performance toolkit. Chrome DevTools is my goto for inbrowser performance analysis. I use the PageSpeed Insights and YSlow extensions for converting performance observations into actions. I love bookmarklets, especially for doing performance analysis in mobile browsers. The websites I run are monitored using several RUM and synthetic performance measurement services.

But I rely on WebPageTest more than all of these other tools combined. Why?

You can run WebPageTest from anywhere. It doesn't require installing anything, all you need is a browser. I've frequently run an analysis of someone's website in IE from China on my iPhone and shown them the results midconversation. They're amazed, and I have to swing the conversation from explaining how such a powerful analysis can be done so quickly on my phone to what they need to do to make their website faster.

WebPageTest makes it easy to save and share results. When analyzing performance, it's often hard for one person to convey their experience to other team members. Sharing a WebPageTest URL ensures that everyone is looking at the same experience. This is especially helpful in bug reports. Since results are never deleted, it's possible to go back to review performance problems in older browsers and previous versions of the website.

WebPageTest covers a wide range of performance metrics. It has waterfall charts with the associated request and response headers. It has timing metrics including time to first byte, document complete, and fully loaded. WebPageTest breaks down the number of requests and bytes by content type. Users who look deeper find the CPU utilization, bandwidth, and main thread timelines, which are often the key for uncovering the most critical performance fixes.

More than anything else, WebPageTest is constantly innovating in the space of web performance. Ten years ago everyone tracked window.onload as a reflection of how long it took for a user to start experiencing a website. And ten years ago that was a satisfactory approximation. But today's websites use AJAX, preloading, async loading, lazyloading, and other advanced techniques, which means we can no longer rely on window.onload to be an accurate reflection of what the user sees.

WebPageTest leads the way in finding new ways to measure and convey the user experience. This started with its focus on filmstrip views and side-by-side videos. Highlighting start render time lets website owners know how long users are waiting to get an indication that the website is even alive and able to respond to their requests. The most important innovation is the development of the Speed Index metric: one number that summarizes the overall rendering experience.

WebPageTest is the leading web performance tool in the world today. It is easy to use, provides the performance metrics that matter, and is pioneering new ways to measure the actual user experience that websites deliver. In 2009's Even Faster Web Sites, I wrote that WebPageTest "hasn't gotten the wide adoption it deserves." Fortunately, that's no longer true. In fact, now there's even a book about it! Read on and find out how to get the most out of WebPageTest to help you deliver a web experience that is fast and enjoyable.

—*Steve Souders, Chief SpeedCurver at SpeedCurve, "working on the interplay between performance and design" - http://stevesouders.com*

Preface

WebPageTest is a synthetic performance testing tool for websites that has evolved since its original public release in 2008. I originally developed it at AOL as a tool to provide developers information on the page load experience for end users (with realistic connectivity and in browsers that were used to visit sites). At the time, most developers used Firefox because the developer tools were much better than what were available in any other browser, and the data center that served the pages was right across the street, connected by fast ethernet to the office. In that environment, all pages loaded unrealistically fast and we needed a way to analyze and share the performance that users experienced in Internet Explorer, on Windows, and in the slow connectivity environments that existed at the time (dialup and slow DSL primarily).

The features, supported browsers, and platforms have evolved over time, but the core mission has been very consistent: to provide detailed information to developers about the loading performance of their pages in a realistic end user environment.

WebPageTest is an open source project on GitHub, available for people to install and use in whatever environment they would like, with a very liberal BSD license. There are several commercial testing platforms that use all or some of the WebPageTest code and it also powers the HTTP Archive (httparchive.org). The most visible instance of WebPageTest is the free, public one at webpagetest.org, which is a great demonstration of the performance community coming together with test locations provided by over fifty companies and individuals. As of September 2015, the public instance of WebPageTest is running 45,000 tests per day and there have been roughly 53 million tests run since it was launched in 2008.

WebPageTest is very much a developer tool, built mostly to help developers identify and solve frontend performance issues, so it can be a bit overwhelming at first, but hugely powerful once you get more familiar with it. I'm extremely grateful to O'Reilly, Andy, Marcel, and Rick for putting this book together to help people get past that hurdle and get the most out of WebPageTest.

—*Patrick Meenan, lead developer and creator of WebPageTest*

Who Should Read This Book

- Independent site owners
- Web developers
- Performance engineers

A Word on Web Performance Today

We all know bad web performance when we see it. When something takes too long to load or become interactive, we start to get bored, impatient, or even angry. The speed —or lack thereof—of a web page has the ability to evoke negative feelings and actions from us. And when we lose interest, have to wait too long, or get mad, we may not behave as expected, which is to consume more content, see more advertisements, or purchase more products.

The Web as a whole is getting measurably slower. Rich media, such as photos and videos, are cheaper to download thanks to faster Internet connections but they are also more prevalent than ever. Expectations of performance are high and the bar is being raised ever higher.

Because you're reading this book, chances are you're not only a user but someone who can do something about this problem. There are many tools at your disposal that specialize in web performance optimizations. However, none is more venerable than WebPageTest.org (*http://www.webpagetest.org/*). WebPageTest is a free, open source web application that audits the speed of web pages. In this book, we will walk you through using this tool to test the performance of web pages so that you can diagnose the signs of slowness and get your users back on track.

Navigating This Book

This book is organized into three primary sections: basic, intermediate, and advanced use cases, each of which corresponds to a different level of familiarity with WebPageTest:

- Basic use cases provide a foundation of testing experience by explaining how to run and interpret simple tests.

- Intermediate use cases have a deeper focus on more sophisticated test scenarios, some of which may require scripted commands to configure how the tests are executed.

- Advanced use cases describe lower-level capabilities typically required by special test environments including the API and private instances.

Conventions Used in This Book

The following typographical conventions are used in this book:

Italic
> Indicates new terms, URLs, email addresses, filenames, and file extensions.

`Constant width`
> Used for program listings, as well as within paragraphs to refer to program elements such as variable or function names, databases, data types, environment variables, statements, and keywords.

`Constant width bold`
> Shows commands or other text that should be typed literally by the user.

`Constant width italic`
> Shows text that should be replaced with user-supplied values or by values determined by context.

 This icon signifies a tip, suggestion, or general note.

This icon indicates a warning or caution.

Using Code Examples

This book is here to help you get your job done. In general, if example code is offered with this book, you may use it in your programs and documentation. You do not need to contact us for permission unless you're reproducing a significant portion of the code. For example, writing a program that uses several chunks of code from this book does not require permission. Selling or distributing a CD-ROM of examples from O'Reilly books does require permission. Answering a question by citing this book and quoting example code does not require permission. Incorporating a significant amount of example code from this book into your product's documentation does require permission.

We appreciate, but do not require, attribution. An attribution usually includes the title, author, publisher, and ISBN. For example: "*Using WebPageTest* by Rick Viscomi, Andy Davies, and Marcel Duran (O'Reilly). Copyright 2015 Rick Viscomi, Andy Davies and Marcel Duran, 978-1-491-90259-2."

If you feel your use of code examples falls outside fair use or the permission given above, feel free to contact us at *permissions@oreilly.com*.

Safari® Books Online

 *Safari Books Online* is an on-demand digital library that delivers expert content in both book and video form from the world's leading authors in technology and business.

Technology professionals, software developers, web designers, and business and creative professionals use Safari Books Online as their primary resource for research, problem solving, learning, and certification training.

Safari Books Online offers a range of plans and pricing for enterprise, government, education, and individuals.

Members have access to thousands of books, training videos, and prepublication manuscripts in one fully searchable database from publishers like O'Reilly Media, Prentice Hall Professional, Addison-Wesley Professional, Microsoft Press, Sams, Que, Peachpit Press, Focal Press, Cisco Press, John Wiley & Sons, Syngress, Morgan Kaufmann, IBM Redbooks, Packt, Adobe Press, FT Press, Apress, Manning, New Riders,

McGraw-Hill, Jones & Bartlett, Course Technology, and hundreds more. For more information about Safari Books Online, please visit us online.

How to Contact Us

Please address comments and questions concerning this book to the publisher:

O'Reilly Media, Inc.
1005 Gravenstein Highway North
Sebastopol, CA 95472
800-998-9938 (in the United States or Canada)
707-829-0515 (international or local)
707-829-0104 (fax)

We have a web page for this book, where we list errata, examples, and any additional information. You can access this page at *http://www.oreilly.com/catalog/0636920033592.do*.

To comment or ask technical questions about this book, send email to *bookquestions@oreilly.com*.

For more information about our books, courses, conferences, and news, see our website at *http://www.oreilly.com*.

Find us on Facebook: *http://facebook.com/oreilly*

Follow us on Twitter: *http://twitter.com/oreillymedia*

Watch us on YouTube: *http://www.youtube.com/oreillymedia*

Acknowledgments

There are many people who helped, encouraged, and cajoled us during the long process of writing this book and we're truly grateful for their support.

Chief amongst those is Pat Meenan, who answered our many questions and guided us as we dug into the fabulous tool he created.

Courtney Nash, Brian Anderson, Shiny Kalapurakkel, Gillian McGarvey at O'Reilly, and Gareth Hughes, Tony Quartarolo, Steve Souders and Tim Kadlec are a few of the others we also owe a debt to.

Writing a book takes time and eats into the other aspects of our lives, so perhaps the biggest thanks we owe is to Corinne, Rick's fiancée, Ligia, Marcel's wife, and Nicki, Andy's wife.

Finally, we'd like to thank you, our readers, as we hope this book encourages you to use WebPageTest, host your own instances, integrate it into your daily development cycle and contribute back so that WebPageTest continues to be one of the best tools for analyzing the performance of web pages.

Basic Use Cases

Imagine for a moment that you have been hired as the new assembly line foreman at Gizmos & Doodads Incorporated, a company that manufactures highly desirable widgets. Your new boss tells you about how slow production has been; orders have been taking twice as long to fulfill and the line has been unable to keep up with what is otherwise a successful increase in business. Your job is to make sure that the line workers can meet demand.

You outline a plan to not only meet demand but also have the factory running at peak efficiency. The first step of your plan is to determine the current rate of production and set goals to measure improvement. The second step is to measure and fine-tune the efficiency of each phase of the operation. Step three, of course, is profit.

In order to find out the production speeds, you implement a widget-counter system that measures how quickly each unit is made. After a week of aggregating information, you determine that the end-to-end time for manufacturing is half as fast as you need it to be to meet the quota. You've confirmed that there is indeed a problem in the performance process, but you still don't know why.

To understand what's wrong, you move to the second step and analyze what each part of the assembly line is doing. You inspect every station for inefficiencies and time how long it takes until the task is completed. Contrary to the continuous collection of data in the first step, this one is more like a snapshot of performance. With this new perspective, you're more easily able to see how the parts work together and consume time.

Armed with concrete performance data and a detailed breakdown of each stage of widget production, you can see a path to reaching the goal of doubling assembly speed. As it turns out, the top and bottom pieces of the widget can be assembled independently and combined at the end, halving the time it takes to build!

This plan is not so different from the way you would approach web performance optimization. After determining the actual speed of your web page, you get an idea of how much faster it needs to be. Then you turn to a breakdown of what the page is actually doing while it loads to figure out ways to achieve the necessary speedup required to meet your goal. These two steps are distinct in methodology because they serve different purposes: finding out how fast a page is, and finding out how to make it faster.

This section will approach the utility of WebPageTest from a beginner's point of view, starting with addressing a couple of ways in which it can be misused. Subsequent chapters dive into the fundamental ways WebPageTest can be used to determine how to make a page faster.

CHAPTER 1

How Fast Is My Page?

The first question to pop into the minds of most people tasked with optimizing the performance of a web page is probably "How fast is it?" As in the story about the factory, understanding the current state of a system is an important first step on the road to optimization. Determining the current speed of a page helps to dictate the severity of the performance problem and sets a baseline from which to improve.

Before diving into WebPageTest for the purpose of getting the one golden number that represents the true speed of your page, take a step back and consider two cautionary points. First, the golden number you seek may not be the metric provided by the tool. If you want to know the speed of a page, you should define exactly what you're trying to measure. Second, even if the tool did report on the metric you care about, it is not necessarily representative of the page's true speed. The true speed is that which the real users of the page experience. Real users live all over the world, use different technologies like device type or browser, and connect to the Internet differently. The true speed of this amalgamation is extremely hard to reflect in a single test.

Measure What Matters

WebPageTest measures the speed of a web page based on the amount of time that has elapsed from the initial page request until the browser fires the load event, sometimes referred to as the *document complete time*. This is the time at which the Document Object Model (DOM) has been created and all images have been downloaded and displayed. For most traditional web pages, the load time is a suitable metric for representing how long a user must wait until the page becomes usable.

One misconception about WebPageTest is that the default metric, load time, is always applicable to the page being tested. Not all web pages are created equal, however, and this metric may not accurately represent the true amount of time users wait.

For example, think about the last time you read a news article online. As the page loaded, what were you waiting for? The most probable answer is that you were waiting for the text content of the article itself. The `DOMContentLoaded` event, also reported by WebPageTest, is like the load event except that it doesn't wait for images to be displayed. The timing of this event may be a more appropriate metric to track because the time to load the ancillary images should not necessarily be taken into account. The default metric is not always the most relevant to the page in test.

For one final example, consider the YouTube video player page. This is not a traditional web page and its content is more elaborate than just text and images. Sometimes, as in this case, custom application-specific metrics are needed to represent the true load time. Users of this page are waiting for the video to play, as opposed to the text appearing or images loading. The page itself needs to tell the browser when the wait is actually over, because the built-in events aren't designed for this particular use case of reporting when the video starts playing.

Application-Specific Metrics

You can log custom application-specific metrics to WebPageTest with the User Timing API. Using the YouTube example, when the video starts to play, that moment in time can be marked with a line of JavaScript:

```
performance.mark('playback-start');
```

WebPageTest will capture these marks and make them available in test results.

Synthetic Versus RUM

Web performance tools tend to be divided based on which big question they answer: "How fast is it?" or "How can it be made faster?" The two classifications of tools are commonly referred to as *synthetic* and *real-user monitoring* (RUM). WebPageTest falls under the synthetic category.

There's a saying that when you have a hammer, all of your problems start to look like nails. Similarly, no one type of web performance tool can answer all of your questions. It's important to distinguish what each type does and how it can be used so that you know when to use the right tool for the job:

Synthetic	RUM
Laboratory-like testing	Measures performance of real users
Low variability, controlled	High variability, unrestricted
Ad hoc tests	Continuous data collection

Tools like WebPageTest are considered to be synthetic because of their artificial testing environments. Akin to a clean room in a laboratory, WebPageTest gives its testers granular control over many of the variables that contribute to performance changes, such as geographic location and type of network connection. By making these variables constant, the root causes of poor frontend performance can be more easily identified and measured.

Unlike the control afforded by synthetic testing, RUM does what its name implies and measures the actual performance real users are experiencing in the wild. The unbridled variations in browsers and bandwidth are all accounted for in the reporting so that each and every user's unique environment is represented. By looking at the raw data, you can draw definitive statistical conclusions. For instance, with access to the performance results, you are able to determine the page-load time for any given percentile. RUM is also considered to be monitoring because data tends to be continuously recorded and streamed to a dashboard. By monitoring performance, developers are able to get instant notification when page speed takes an unexpected turn; a decline in speed could theoretically page an engineer immediately if necessary. This is especially useful for mission-critical applications for which performance is just as important as availability.

For attempting to determine the overall speed of a page, it's clear that RUM is the appropriate solution because it accurately represents the performance of actual users. When starting out with WebPageTest, one pitfall is to assume that the synthetic results are like real-user metrics. The reality, however, is that synthetic tools are deliberately designed to focus on the performance of a web page under strict conditions that are otherwise highly volatile in real-user performance.

To help illustrate this pitfall, imagine that you run a synthetic test of your home page and come to find that the load time is 10 seconds. "That's crazy," you think, because it never feels that slow to you. Your real-world experience does not coincide with the test results. It's not that the test is necessarily wrong. The test configuration is meant to represent one particular use case. If it isn't set up to match your browser, in your city, over your connection speed, you're unlikely to get comparable results. The test is only an artificial representation of what someone under similar conditions might experience. It's up to you to configure the test in a way that mimics the conditions that you want to compare. Throughout the book, we'll look at different use cases that each has its own unique conditions, which in turn have corresponding configurations.

CHAPTER 2

What's Slowing Down My Page?

It's good to know how fast a page is. Knowing how to make it faster is even better. Knowing the change in performance over time is extremely important to validating that the optimizations to the page are actually working. Before any optimizations can be made, however, you need to understand how the page is put together and what opportunities exist for optimization. To get there, this chapter will walk you through the steps of running a very simple test and analyzing the results to figure out what exactly is going on under the hood.

Running a Simple Test

Almost everyone who starts out with WebPageTest goes through the home page, which acts as the gateway to the rest of the tool. Putting ourselves in the shoes of someone who has never used the tool before, let's try to run our first test.

First, go to *www.webpagetest.org*. One of the most prominent parts of the page is the great big text-input field, with a prompt to Enter a Website URL (Figure 2-1). Let's get started by providing the web address of a page we want to test (Figure 2-2).

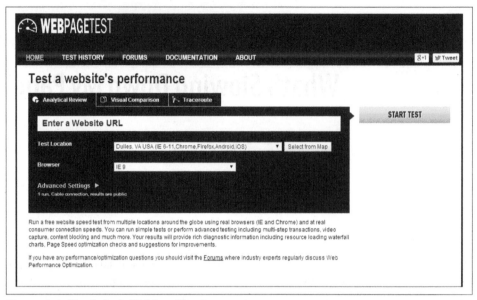

Figure 2-1. The default WebPageTest home page

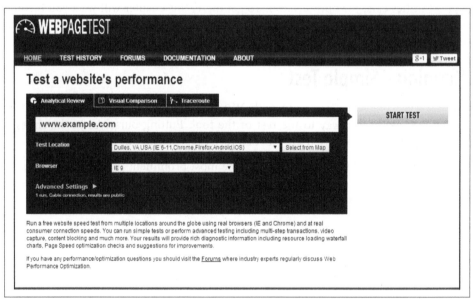

Figure 2-2. The URL field of the home page set to www.example.com

At this point, you may either be feeling overwhelmed by all of the other configuration options or eager to jump in and start customizing the test. Either way, don't worry about the rest of the options. Part II will look at some of the more advanced ways to configure tests. But for our first test, let's simply start with a URL and see what happens when we leave everything else to its default value. To run the test, click on the big Start Test button next to the URL input field. That's it. That's how to run the simplest test with WebPageTest. Now the fun begins.

By now, you've been taken to a page that shows how the test is progressing (Figure 2-3). There are three phases in the lifetime of a test: waiting, testing, and done.

Figure 2-3. The test has progressed to the second phase and is in the process of being run

WebPageTest is a publicly accessible tool, which implies that many people may be trying to use it at the same time. The browser and location are shared commodities, and there could be a queue of tests backed up. This is the waiting phase, when the resource you need is already in use and there may be more tests ahead of you waiting for the same. This can be the most unpredictable phase because of two factors: the variable number of tests in the queue and the variable complexity of the tests. Some tests require more time to complete than others. Having many of these kinds of tests in the queue can slow down this phase to minutes or even hours. Sometimes, a test can get stuck and nothing in the queue can move until an administrator becomes available to sort it out.

 To get an idea of resource availability, check out *webpagetest.org/getLocations.php*. This page lists the available resources for a given location and browser, which you can use to pick a lesser-utilized configuration for faster testing.

If you find yourself in a queue that's not moving, consider changing to a different browser or test location. Each combination has its own queue, and this tool will tell you which ones are the shortest.

When your test has reached the front of the queue, it will switch to the testing phase. At this point, a browser somewhere is loading the web page you entered and collecting lots of data. Because we configured a very basic test, this phase should only take a minute. Finally, when the test reaches completion, the progress page becomes a report summary (Figure 2-4). This is where we can start to analyze the performance of our page.

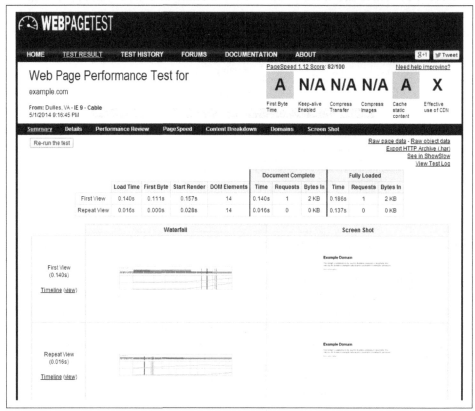

Figure 2-4. After the test has completed, the test progress page turns into the test summary page, which provides an overview of the page performance

The first place to look is the table of data. This is the metrics summary of the test, containing a breakdown of important milestones of the page-load process. From left to right:

Load Time
> The time from the initial request until the browser load event. Also known as the *document complete time*. This is the default performance metric on WebPageTest.

First Byte
> Time until the server responds with the first byte of the response.

Start Render
> Time until the browser paints content to the screen.

DOM Elements
> Number of elements in the document.

Document Complete

> *Time*
> > Same as Load Time.

> *Requests*
> > Number of HTTP requests before the load event, not including the initial request.

> *Bytes In*
> > Total size of the Document Complete Requests' response bodies in bytes.

Fully Loaded

> *Time*
> > The time from the initial request until WebPageTest determines that the page has finished loading content. The page might have waited for the load event to defer loading secondary content. The time it takes to load the secondary content is accounted for in the Fully Loaded Time.

> *Requests*
> > Total number of HTTP requests recorded in this test run, not including the initial request.

> *Bytes In*
> > Total number of bytes received in this test run.

Before each test, WebPageTest clears the browser cache to ensure that it downloads all resources. This is considered to be the *first view*, representing a new user visiting the page without any local copies of the resources. One of the default WebPageTest configurations is to load the page a second time without clearing the browser cache; this is known as the *repeat view*. The difference between the number of requests of first and repeat views is an indicator of the number of cacheable resources on the page. The metrics for each view are enumerated in the summary table.

In addition to the first and repeat views, WebPageTest has another configuration for the number of times to run the test. By default, this value is 1. The summary metrics only reflect the performance of the single test run. With so few runs, these metrics can easily be affected by network or server fluctuations. Anomalies do happen, and only running one test can disguise the anomalies as realities. One WebPageTest best practice is to run tests multiple times and choose the most representative run to look at. Tests can be run up to nine times (not including repeat views). The method for choosing the most representative test run is to sort all runs by some metric and choose the middle-most run. By definition, this is referred to as the *median run*. The default median metric is the document complete time or load time.

There exists a URL parameter named *medianMetric*. Change the metric used to calculate the median run by providing the `medianMetric` URL parameter. Set its value to one of the other metrics' names, and the summary metrics will reflect this other run. For example, `?medianMetric=bytesIn` (*http://www.webpaget est.org/result/140603_1J_633/?medianMetric=bytesIn*) chooses the median based on the number of bytes downloaded. See "Details of Requests In Test Results" on page 171 for a full list of median metric options.

After running this simple test, we're able to report on the summary metrics to get an idea of how fast or slow the page performance was. Keep in mind, though, that the performance of the test may not be representative of the actual performance live users of the page are experiencing. The real value in these metrics comes from comparing them against the performance of other similarly configured tests. Comparison is the key to determining whether the differences between tests have made a positive or negative impact. This first test won't do much good unless we're able to find ways to optimize the page and rerun the test for comparison, so in the next section we will look at how to read the waterfall diagram to find out what could be slowing the page down.

Reading a Waterfall

Undeniably, the most important part of a web performance report is the waterfall diagram. Waterfalls are a visualization of the network activity, which is broken down into individual HTTP requests (see Figure 2-5).

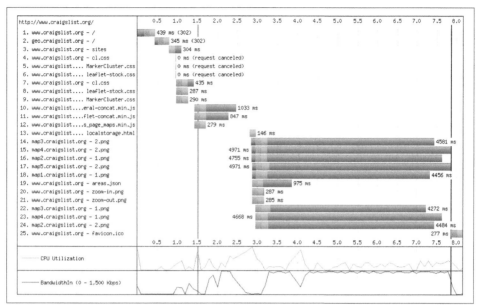

Figure 2-5. An example of a waterfall

Each request is made up of five main phases:

DNS lookup

The time to resolve a human-friendly hostname like *http://www.example.com* to its *Internet Protocol* (IP) address. An IP address is like a phone number unique to the computer that will be serving the web page. Resolving the DNS of a web page is sort of like looking through a phone book.

Initial connection

The time for the browser to establish a connection to the server. If resolving the DNS of the server is like looking up a phone number, this is the step of dialing the number and waiting for someone to answer.

SSL negotiation

The time for the browser and server to agree on a secure way to communicate. This step is skipped for plain HTTP requests but is a requirement for secure protocols like HTTPS and SPDY.

Time to First Byte (TTFB)

The time for the server to prepare the response to the request. Prior to this phase, the server had no idea what the request was even for. This is when the server looks something up in a database or calls an external API.

Content download

The time for the server to send the entire contents of the response. This time is directly proportional to the size of the response and the speed of the connection.

Figure 2-6 shows a request with all of the previously listed phases.

Figure 2-6. An example of a request with all five phases: DNS lookup (teal), initial connection (orange), SSL negotiation (purple), TTFB (green), and content download (blue)

Waterfalls are also decorated with bars and lines, marking the times at which page-level events occur, as shown in Figure 2-7.

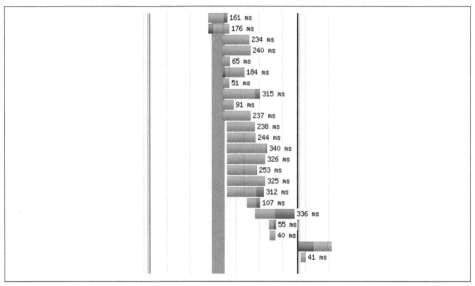

Figure 2-7. The waterfall events shown behind the requests. From left to right: msFirstPaint (light green), Start Render (dark green), DOM Content Loaded (pink), Document Complete (dark blue), and On Load (light blue)

There are four basic page-level events:

Start Render (first paint)

The time for the browser to display the first pixel of content (paint) on the screen. There are two separate events shown, one for each method of measurement. Start Render is WebPageTest's own metric, determined by programmatically watching for visual changes to the page. This is illustrated in the section "Filmstrip and Video" on page 41. The other metric is reported by the browser and represents the time it claims to have first painted to the screen.

DOM Content Loaded

After the browser has received the HTML payload, it parses it into the DOM, which is a virtual representation of the page structure. The browser will fire an event to let the page know that the DOM is ready so that the page can go on to interact with it. One such interaction, for example, would be to assign a click-event listener to a button. This page-level event has both a start and end time, representing how long the page spent handling the DOM ready event.

On Load

The start and end time of the page's load-event handler. The browser fires the load event when the DOM is ready and all images have loaded. Pages typically use this event handler to perform secondary tasks like loading content below the fold (outside of the user's viewport).

Document Complete

Effectively, the time that the browser fires the load event. This event name can be considered a misnomer because the document may not necessarily be complete. Around this time, the page's script is hard at work in the load-event handler firing off more requests for secondary content. The incomplete nature of this metric is why Fully Loaded was added to the table of metrics from the previous section.

The final type of waterfall adornment is the request highlighting. Yellow and red highlights are applied to request rows to indicate that some kind of inefficiency or error occurred.

Highlights fall into three main categories:

Errors (red)

The most common cause for this is likely to be HTTP 404 errors (Not Found), which can occur if the URL of a resource was mistyped or if the resource was deleted from the server. Other typical errors include HTTP 500 internal server errors, when the server can't respond to the request because of a bug in its own code. See Figure 2-8.

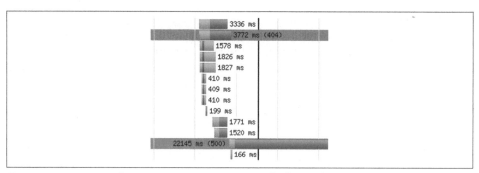

Figure 2-8. A series of requests, two responses to which are shown as errors: HTTP 404 (Not Found) and 500 (Internal Server Error)

Redirects (yellow)

A resource was requested at one particular URL and the server reported that it does exist, but under a different URL. The alternate URL is returned and the browser has to try again. These are HTTP 301 and 302 response codes (Figure 2-9 and Figure 2-10). This is inefficient because the browser had to repeat its request, further delaying the time to load the resource. Redirects commonly occur when the server rewrites the URL of the page, such as from *example.com* to *www.example.com*. Secure web pages may even redirect users from *http://exam ple.com* to *https://example.com*. Or even worse, both: *http://example.com* to *http:// www.example.com* to *https://www.example.com*. These redirects occur on the initial request before any content has even been loaded, so they are considered especially harmful to page performance.

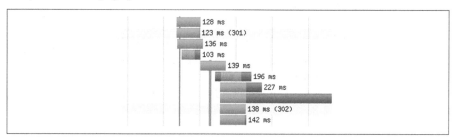

Figure 2-9. A series of requests, two responses to which are shown as redirects: HTTP 301 (Moved Permanently) and 302 (Found)

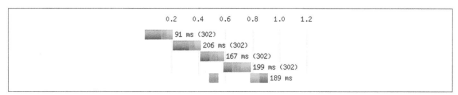

Figure 2-10. The initial request for a page is redirected four times in a chain reaction of redirection. The initial request is already at a 800 millisecond disadvantage. This happens when the server tries to rewrite a page URL, commonly to a different sub-domain or protocol, which in turn causes another rewrite, and so on, until finally the actual resource is able to load.

Cache (yellow)

In repeat views, which is the second pass of a page with the browser cache already warmed up, some resources have been downloaded but didn't include information about how long they are valid. For each of these resources, the browser had to ask the server if what it has in cache is still valid. The server responded with an HTTP 304 code (Not Modified) to answer that the file has not been changed since it was cached, as shown in Figure 2-11. Having a resource in cache is always better than having to download it all over again, but this 304 response should not be necessary. When the server sent the resource to the browser the first time, it should have included all of the pertinent information of its cache lifetime.

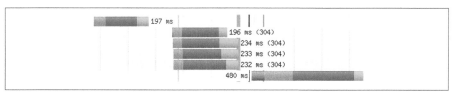

Figure 2-11. A series of requests, four responses to which are shown as 304 (Not Modified)

Waterfall Slope

In addition to the lines, bars, and colors in a waterfall diagram, there's another, more subtle indicator. Remember that the start offset is the amount of time that has passed since the page started loading until the request is finally made. Waterfall shapes are determined by the start offsets of the requests. Shapes can be tall, short, wide, or narrow depending on the number of requests and the rate at which they are completed. See Figure 2-12 and Figure 2-13 as examples of these variations. Identifying the shape of a waterfall is an easy way to see the performance big picture.

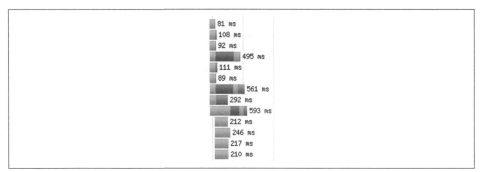

Figure 2-12. An example of a series of requests in a waterfall with tall and narrow slope. Many requests are initiated at roughly the same time, as illustrated by their mostly aligned left edges.

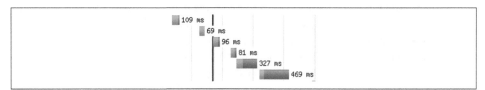

Figure 2-13. An example of a series of requests in a waterfall with short and wide slope. Several requests are made in a row but with a noticeable amount of time between them. The horizontal slope here is an indicator of inefficient network utilization.

Waterfall shapes are simply a general descriptor for a page's performance. To really understand which requests are hurting performance, we need to look at the waterfall's slope. Recall from geometry that the slope of a line in a coordinate system is its height divided by its length, or "rise over run." In a waterfall diagram, things are a little different. The top-left point is the origin (or zero value), so increasing requests actually go downward. Still, we can apply the concept of slope to waterfalls in order to better understand them.

Looking at a waterfall from the perspective of request start offsets, you can begin to notice similarities and differences. For example, many requests in a row with close to the same start offset appear stacked. If you draw a line to the left of the requests, the line will look almost vertical, as shown in Figure 2-14. In terms of slope, this is ideal. What it means is that in a given period of time, many things were happening. The opposite would be a case when adjacent requests have very different start offsets, in which case the slope line would be long and approaching horizontal. These imaginary near-horizontal lines are excellent indicators of poor performance afoot. In essence, something is happening such that requests are getting delayed.

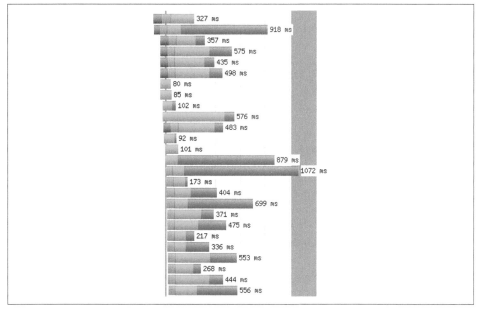

Figure 2-14. An example of a long series of requests in a waterfall with tall slope. These are mostly images loading over five domain shards. The vertical slope is an indicator of efficient use of the network.

There are a couple of key considerations when looking at waterfall slopes. First, be aware of the scale of the time axis. Tests that run in a short amount of time may sometimes be shown in units of half a second, which would exaggerate the horizontal aspect of slope. Second, keep in mind which requests are most important to the user experience. Many requests may be necessary to construct a usable page. The *critical path* is the name for the requests that are required to get the page to this state. The slope of the critical path should always be as vertical as possible. In contrast, the slope of requests outside of the critical path should be second in priority.

You can restrict which requests appear in the waterfall diagram on the Customize Waterfall page, a link to which is accessible directly under the waterfall. Enter ranges of request numbers to narrow it down. This is especially useful for limiting the waterfall to only the critical path.

Connection View

To recap, the waterfall diagram is a visualization of the network traffic while a given page loads. This view is great for spotting most performance anti-patterns related to the critical path. WebPageTest provides an alternate view, called the *connection view*, focused not on the sequence of requests but rather the connections through which requests are made (Figure 2-15). This type of view lends itself to better illustrating how the networking between server and browser works.

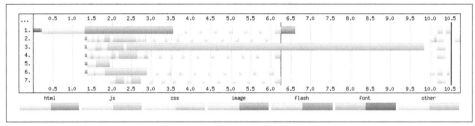

Figure 2-15. The connection view for a page with many JavaScript resources, as indicated by the color coding. Each row is numbered 1 through 7, representing seven total connections. Each connection would normally be labeled with the host to which it is connecting, but this information has been omitted from the figure for simplicity.

Each row in the connection view diagram represents a communication channel established over the Transmission Control Protocol (TCP). It's not uncommon to see multiple connections opened for the same domain. When this happens, requests are able to be made in parallel, which can be useful for taking advantage of available bandwidth. Note, however, that with multiplexing support in HTTP/2, it is no longer necessary or beneficial to open multiple connections. A single connection can efficiently stream multiple responses concurrently.

Drawn in each row is one or more requests. Although the requests are illustrated differently from the waterfall diagram, keep in mind that the same data is being shown in the connection view. The DNS lookup, initial connection, and SSL negotiation phases are shown as short bars before the first request in each row. By definition, each row has one and only one initial connection. Further, each domain has one and only one row that completes the DNS resolution phase. This illustrates the reuse of phases between subsequent requests to the same domain. The domain name does not need to be resolved again, plus open connections can be reused without penalty of creating another.

The TTFB and content download phases are included, but their colors are unique to the content type of the request. For example, JavaScript resources are tan and images are purple. The legend below the diagram shows what each color represents. The lighter shade is the TTFB and the darker shade is the content download phase. Be aware that very small resources may have download times so small that the darker shade is virtually imperceptible. All of this color coding has nothing to do with connections, but it still adds some value to the diagram by making it easier to spot patterns and irregularities.

Common Anti-Patterns

So far, we've looked at ways of reading a waterfall to conclude that something is wrong. But to figure out *what* is wrong, you need to know what you're looking for. Some performance problems have a telltale signature, called an *anti-pattern*, that they leave behind in a waterfall. Spotting these anti-patterns takes some practice, so in this section we'll look at a few common performance issues and their signatures.

Long first-byte time

If we're going to look at common performance issues, let's start with the one that people seem to need a lot of help with. A tweet in December 2012 by WebPageTest creator Pat Meenan, stated that 90% of the posts on the tool's forums had to do with excessive time-to-first-byte results. At the beginning of this chapter we defined First Byte as the time from the request to the first byte of the response. This isn't to be conflated with the Time to First Byte (TTFB), which is one of a few phases of the initial request that can contribute to unacceptable first-byte times.

Starting from the beginning, DNS resolution could be affected by long certificate chains or high latency on the name servers. Long DNS resolution could be debugged using free online tools. The connection phase of the initial request could be compromised by inefficient server settings, such as a small congestion window, which would result in more round-trips than necessary. The security negotiation phase requires even more round-trips between the browser and server to secure the connection. Despite everything that can go wrong in the first three phases, the TTFB phase tends to be the culprit, as shown in Figure 2-16. This is the phase affected by long-running server processing, typically database access. Because the server is outside of WebPageTest's instrumentation reach, diagnosing backend issues will require additional tooling.

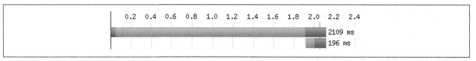

Figure 2-16. A 2,109 millisecond request with a 1,795 millisecond TTFB, which accounts for approximately 85% of the total request time. The subsequent request is blocked during the entire TTFB phase.

This anti-pattern is arguably one of the most detrimental because it affects the initial response, which contains the markup and styles necessary to draw something onto the screen. Users waiting for the response would have no visual fodder to alleviate the wait. Anti-patterns after the first paint would at least leave something on screen for users to preoccupy themselves with, unlike this one. This first request's performance impacts the lower limit on how fast the page can get. No amount of optimization on the frontend can change how quickly the backend is able to service requests.

Reopened connections

One of the easiest anti-patterns to spot in the connection view is the problem of not reusing connections. In order for the browser to request a resource from the server, it needs to have an open connection, or channel, over which to make the request. These channels are usually left open for the browser to reuse for its next requests. This is accomplished by the server instructing the browser how long the connection is good for. Without it, the browser must initiate a new connection for each and every request, as shown in Figure 2-17. The underlying connection protocol, TCP, is known as the *three-way handshake* for the number of messages between browser and server. So for every request, additional time-consuming round-trips are unnecessarily incurred. This is made worse for secure requests, which require even more round-trips for the SSL negotiation phase. Reused connections share the preexisting security, avoiding the need to spend redundant time establishing another channel. Enabling connection reuse requires a change to the web-server configuration; the Keep-Alive setting must be turned on. Fortunately, this is an easy and well-documented change.

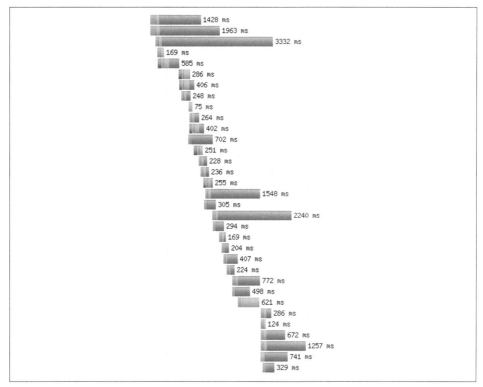

Figure 2-17. Looking closely, you can see that many of these requests start with a small orange bar to indicate that new connections are being made. This is time that could otherwise be spent downloading the requested content.

Closing connections is the signature anti-pattern of the connection view. By design, each row is a connection, so you'd normally expect to see connections to the primary content server being reused for multiple requests, leading to many resources shown side-by-side. For this anti-pattern, however, connections are used only once, so each row would only contain a single request. This problem is unique to each server, so it may not be a problem throughout the entire diagram.

Canceled requests

Consider a page with relatively complex markup consisting of many elements, several levels deep. This page was built with some best practices in mind, so the script tags were appended to the body of the document. After making the initial request for this page, a simple browser would receive the response data and linearly parse the document to construct the DOM. As it parses further and deeper into the markup, more time passes before those footer scripts are loaded. Finally, after everything above the scripts is parsed, the scripts can be requested from the server. If this seems inefficient, that's because it is. Modern browsers are smarter than that, so they use a technique to find resources like these scripts earlier, but not always without making a mistake.

Modern browsers employ lookahead scanning on a page to get a sense of what will need to be loaded. Think of it as two parsers on the document at the same time: one does the simple job of parsing the markup into the DOM, and the other—known as the *lookahead pre-parser*—jumps ahead to find external resources that will be needed by the page. When the lookahead pre-parser finds one such resource, it tries to download it as soon as possible. The problem is that the DOM may contain information relevant to that resource, which may not have been parsed yet. If this happens, the lookahead pre-parser will have wastefully started loading a resource that cannot be used anymore, and WebPageTest will record this as a canceled request. Canceled requests will eventually be completed later, resulting in a duplicate entry in the waterfall diagram.

This problem, mostly limited to Internet Explorer, happens because the lookahead pre-parser makes some incorrect assumptions about the resources it's trying to preload. For example, if a script source attribute is given a relative file path like /main.js, the lookahead pre-parser may see this and assume that the file is relative to the current host. However, there is a way to override the host to use for relative paths in HTML; this is known as the *base tag*. If content is served over *www.example.com*, the base tag can be used to supplant the host with something else, like *foo.example.com*, where all relative file paths should be served. If the lookahead pre-parser gets to the *main.js* script before the DOM parser finds the base tag, it will incorrectly look for the resource at *www.example.com/main.js*. Even if a resource exists at that location, it's still not what the document actually requested and it must be discarded. Similarly, other kinds of markup can invalidate preloaded resources like the charset and x-ua-compatible meta tags. As is the situation with the base tag, these tags can lead to invalid assumptions about the resources to be loaded on the page.

Canceled requests have noticeable effects on the performance of a web page. The resources that the lookahead pre-parser was trying to preload may have been unnecessarily competing for bandwidth with other important resources on the page (Figure 2-18). Worse, when the resources are finally loaded, they may come through seconds after the initial attempt.

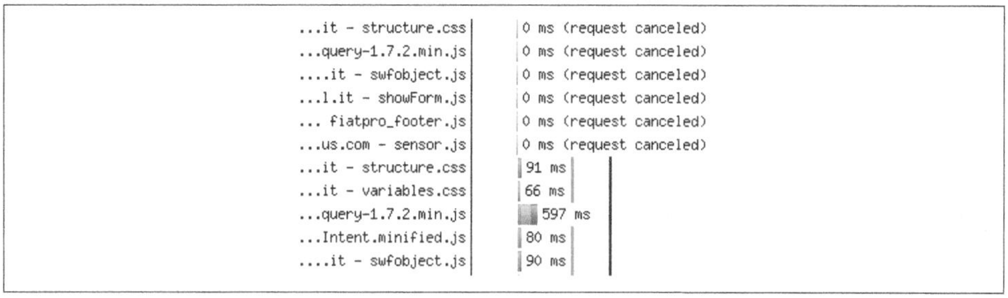

```
       ...it - structure.css |  0 ms (request canceled)
    ...query-1.7.2.min.js |  0 ms (request canceled)
       ....it - swfobject.js |  0 ms (request canceled)
       ...l.it - showForm.js |  0 ms (request canceled)
       ... fiatpro_footer.js |  0 ms (request canceled)
       ...us.com - sensor.js |  0 ms (request canceled)
       ...it - structure.css |  91 ms
        ...it - variables.css |  66 ms
     ...query-1.7.2.min.js |  597 ms
       ...Intent.minified.js |  80 ms
        ....it - swfobject.js |  90 ms
```

Figure 2-18. Requests for several resources are shown as canceled. Many of the subsequent requests are for the same resources, duplicating effort.

Fortunately, there are some best practices that can help you avoid this situation. Meta tags with equivalent attributes to HTTP response headers should be set as a header to begin with. This avoids preload invalidation because the lookahead pre-parser knows to make the correct assumptions before the DOM parser even begins. As for the base tag, if it must be used, it should be included as early in the HTML head element as possible. This will reduce the amount of time that the lookahead pre-parser has to make incorrect assumptions, but it is not bulletproof.

Network silence

Maintaining good waterfall slope requires the number of requests in a given time to be high. Of the anti-patterns that kill slope, network silence is the epitome of suboptimal request scheduling. A silent network means that requests are not being made. This is fine if the page has finished loading, but when there are still outstanding resources, they should be loaded as soon as possible. The observable clues to network silence are long pauses or gaps between requests in the waterfall, low bandwidth utilization, and, more rarely, high CPU utilization.

An inverse relationship between CPU and bandwidth during a period of network silence is usually indicative of a blocking process. Because the browser's main thread is busy on a long-running process, it is unable to proceed with other jobs in the queue, such as fetching additional resources. There are a couple of ways that a web application can hold up the queue like this. Most commonly, slow JavaScript is to blame. Scripts that do too much, like iterating over a very large list and processing each item, will take a noticeably long time to complete, as shown in Figure 2-19. When this happens, the browser is unable to respond to user input, including click or scroll events. One technique to mitigate this effect is to yield the thread back to the browser by using requestAnimationFrame or setTimeout to delay additional processing after the script has run for some time. Complicated markup can also take a long time to process. For example, using HTML tables for layout has often been discouraged because of its lack of semantics. Using tables for layout could also be computationally expensive, due to the high cost of laying out a table that changes size to fit its content. This can be avoided by using less expensive markup for layout. Also keep in mind that the impacts of slow JavaScript and complicated markup are exacerbated on a slower CPU.

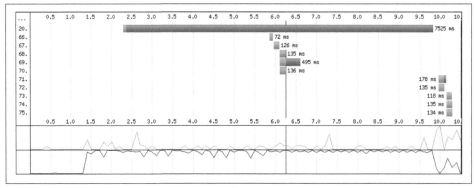

Figure 2-19. In this abbreviated waterfall, the gap between request numbers 70 and 71 is nearly four seconds long. The low CPU and high bandwidth utilizations suggest that request 20 is likely to blame for blocking request 71.

As easy as it is to see network silence in a waterfall diagram, WebPageTest is not equipped to identify the underlying problem by default. As with the problem of a long first-byte time, the tool is great at showing that there is a problem but additional tools are necessary to determine what the problem actually is. In the case of network silence, a profiler is required.

WebPageTest Grades

Similar to YSlow, the web performance analysis browser plug-in developed by Yahoo!, the WebPageTest grades evaluate the page data captured by the test and show whether the page has passed or failed a certain goal. There are several goals being tested, all of which were chosen to be the most essential performance benchmarks. For example, YSlow or Google's Page Speed tool might give a grade for combining multiple stylesheets into one. In reality, there can be valid reasons for loading multiple stylesheets, yet these tools aren't necessarily able to take that into consideration. The WebPageTest grades, on the other hand, are a set of web performance must-haves to which most, if not all, pages should adhere. In this section, we'll look at how the grades are evaluated and what you can do to improve them.

In general, grades are evaluated first as a percentage. The numeric values are converted to the familiar letter grades on a standard academic scale:

Letter Grade	Percentage
A:	90%+
B:	80–89%
C:	70–79%
D:	60–69%
F:	0–59%

The intention of the grades described in this section is to call attention to some of the most important web performance best practices. The grades are organized so that the most critical appear first. This means that you should focus your efforts on optimizing things like connection reuse and *gzipping* before moving on to other important but less impactful optimizations like image compression or content delivery networks.

First-Byte Time

The first-byte time is the time at which the browser receives the first byte of the HTML content. This grade rates how tolerable the first-byte time is for the test. Up until this time, the only things going on are the network-level connections and the server-side processing. As a reminder, these phases are the DNS lookup, initial TCP connection, SSL negotiation (where applicable), and TTFB. WebPageTest rates a test's first-byte time by looking at how long these phases take in aggregate and comparing it against a target time. The closer to the target time, the better the rating.

The formula to compute the grade of the test is based on the expected number of round-trips between browser and server. The grade automatically fails if the first-byte time is greater than seven round-trips plus some allowance time. The target time is expected to be three round-trips plus allowance time for SSL negotiation:

```
target first-byte time = RTT * 3 + SSL
```

If the initial connection is less than three seconds, RTT = initial connection. Otherwise, RTT is the network shaping latency time (i.e., 28 ms for Cable) plus 100 ms. See the section "Traffic Shaping" on page 77 for more on customizing the connection speed.

The percentage value for this grade is evaluated by the following formula:

```
value = 100 - ((observed first-byte time - target first-byte time) / 10)
```

For demonstration purposes, let's evaluate the first-byte time for a hypothetical test. The first-byte phases of the initial request are:

- 100 ms DNS lookup
- 150 ms initial connection
- 500 ms TTFB

The target first-byte time would be three times the initial connection, or 450 ms. The observed first-byte time (the sum of the phases) is 750 ms, which is 300 ms slower than the target time. That would make the value 70, resulting in a C grade.

```
target first-byte time = 3 * initial connection = 3 * 150 ms = 450 ms
observed first-byte time = 100 ms + 150 ms + 500 ms = 750 ms
value = 100 - ((750 ms - 450 ms) / 10) = 100 - (300 / 10) = 100 - 30 = 70
```

In this way, WebPageTest does a good job of highlighting the opportunity for optimizing the first-byte time. At a glance, it should be easy to see that the initial request TTFB is dragging the grade down.

Keep-Alive Enabled

The grade for enabling Keep-Alive measures the effectiveness of connection reuse. As we've seen in the "Reopened connections" on page 20 anti-pattern section, closing connections are a missed opportunity for performance enhancement. Necessitating additional round-trips between the user and the server to initiate a connection is redundant and time-consuming. The purpose of this grade is to evaluate the extent to which requests are inefficiently reopening connections.

Recall that a connection *must* be made whenever the page is communicating with a new host. For example, a page with two resources from a single host should ideally make a connection for the request for the first resource and reuse that same connection for the second resource. We say that the page has two requests to the same host, the first of which is expected to negotiate a connection and the second of which is expected to communicate using the already-open channel.

The grade is evaluated according to the following formula:

```
value = number of reused connections / expected number of reused connections
```

Let's look at another hypothetical test to see how the grade would be evaluated. The requests per host are:

- 1 request to Host A
- 10 requests to Host B
- 7 requests to Host C

The expected number of reused connections can be expressed as the total number of requests less one initial connection per host. That would make 15 reused connections. Hypothetically, however, Host B is the only one that has the Keep-Alive configuration enabled. Hence, the number of reused connections would only be Host B's requests (10) less the initial connection: 9. Therefore the value would be 9/15, or 60%, equal to a barely passing grade of D. In other words, 60% of the requests could have shaved a round-trip's worth of time off simply for reusing the existing open connection.

Compress Transfer

Like Keep-Alive, compressing text-based resources over the network is a straightforward server-side configuration. When enabled, resources like HTML, JavaScript, and CSS files will be compressed, or gzipped, resulting in a smaller file size and quicker download. The grade for compression is also like that for enabling Keep-Alive in that it is a ratio of the actual performance over the expected performance.

The exact formula for this grade is:

```
value = optimized resource size / actual resource size
```

To determine the optimized resource size, WebPageTest actually compresses each and every resource to find out if it is suitably smaller than the size of the resource as it was transferred. "Suitably smaller" in this case means that the resource is more than 10% smaller and more than 1,400 bytes when compressed. If a resource meets these conditions, the test is penalized in proportion to the number of bytes that could have been saved.

Note that because images are binary resources, they are excluded from the compression grading. But they are not exempt from scrutiny, as the following two grades are especially for them.

Compress Images

Just as text-based files can be gzipped to save bytes and time, images are compressable as well. WebPageTest specifically evaluates JPEG images by optimizing them and measuring the difference. A test is penalized if it contains images that can be reduced in size by configuring them to load progressively and degrading visual quality to 85%. The exact evaluation is:

```
value = optimized image size / actual image size
```

After compressing each image, its size is compared to the actual image without optimizations. The greater the difference, the lower the score. For example, if 1 MB of images could be compressed by 150 KB, the optimized image size would be ~85% of the actual size, resulting in a grade of B.

Progressive JPEGs

JPEG images are one of two types: baseline or progressive. Most images used on the web are baseline, which appear to load from top to bottom. Progressive JPEGs, on the other hand, show the entire image with low quality at first, and then with gradually increasing quality. The advantage of the progressive JPEG type is that the user perceives it as loading more quickly, even if it is of low quality. As we'll discuss in "Perceived Performance" on page 39, giving users the perception of speed is a very valuable optimization.

This grade is evaluated by the ratio of the number of progressive bytes in a JPEG to its total size:

```
value = progressive bytes / total bytes
```

The WebPageTest grading is based on 10 KB chunks of the image, each of which is checked for a new scan. Scans are the gradual increases of quality. If the chunk contains a scan, all 10 KB are considered to be progressive bytes. All of the test's JPEGs are checked and the bytes are tallied to come up with a final value, which is then expressed as a letter grade.

Cache Static Content

Static resources like images tend not to change often. Repeated visits to a page may be redundantly downloading these resources if they are not properly configured to stay in the browser's cache. This grade checks the HTTP responses for resources that are determined to be static and evaluates them based on their lifetime:

```
value = expiration score / number of static resources
```

This formula is a little different from the previous grades, as it relies on a scoring system. The way it works is that a static resource's response headers are inspected for a cache lifetime value. This could come from a Cache-Control: max-age or Expires header. A static resource is given a score of 100 if its lifetime is greater than a week. If not, it can still be redeemed for 50 points if its lifetime is greater than an hour. Otherwise, it receives a score of 0. The scores for all static resources are tallied and divided by the total number of static resources to get the percent value.

Effective Use of CDNs

A *content delivery network* (CDN) is a system for distributing resources to servers geographically closer to users. One benefit of this is that the round-trip time is faster. The formula is straightforward:

```
value = static resources served from a known CDN / number of static resources
```

WebPageTest keeps a log of known CDN providers. Each static resource is checked to see if its host server was one such provider. The more resources served from a CDN, the better the value. This grade is unique in that there are only two possible outcomes: pass or fail. The passing grade for using a CDN effectively is to have at least 80% of static resources served from a CDN.

CHAPTER 3

Cache Optimization

There's no question that the longer a web page takes to load, the less attention a user will give it. Curious minds might wonder what happens to users' attention as a web page becomes faster. How fast can something get without users noticing that they had to wait for it? Research shows that, in general, people perceive load times of 100 milliseconds or less as seemingly instantaneous. This is the Holy Grail of web performance; if we could make a web page load faster than a user can notice, our work here would be done. Easy, right? Not quite.

Think about everything that could go wrong while a page loads. Before the server can even send the first bit of data, a few round-trips' worth of negotiation take place just to open the lines for communication. Each phase in the connection chips away at the 100-millisecond budget for which we've aimed. It's not long before the users notice that they're waiting on us to load the page. Caching to the rescue.

What is a *cache*? A textbook definition might be that a cache is just a portion of computer memory temporarily set aside for data needed in the near future. Conceptually, caching allows an application to quickly access data. The canonical example of caching is saving the results of CPU computations in random-access memory (RAM) as opposed to disk space. The time required to read from and write to disk is much greater than it is with memory, so effective caching can have profound impacts on computation time. Even newer technology like solid state drives (SSDs) are slower to use than RAM due to hardware limitations.

Instead of a CPU, RAM, and persistent storage drives, we're concerned with users, their browsers, and our web server. Analogously, a user needs to fetch information and instead of taking the long and slow route to our server, the user would simply be able to access a local copy minus the waiting. With the browser's cache, we are able to save copies of resources like images, stylesheets, and scripts directly on the user's machine. The next time one of these resources is needed, it can be served from cache instead of taking the slower journey across the Internet.

Of course, there are limitations to the cache. Most important, it has a finite size. Modern browsers' caches are in the tens of megabytes, which may be enough to comfortably fit an average-sized website. But the browser cache is shared among all websites. There is bound to be a congestion issue. When this happens, the browser performs an *eviction*. One or more unlucky resources are removed from the cache to make room for new ones. Another consideration is that resources are not expected to be valid indefinitely; each resource is saved along with metadata about how long the browser can consider it to be fresh. Even if a resource is in the cache and the user makes a request for that same resource, it may be served over the network if the cached version is not fresh.

We'll explore the concept of freshness later in this chapter and provide details of how to configure resources efficiently for caching. We will also look at the tools WebPageTest provides to measure how effectively a website uses browser caching.

Enabling Repeat View

Tests that run on WebPageTest default to a "cold" cache experience much like that of a user who has never been to a website before. This allows the tool to record the network activity of all resources needed to build the page. The test browser follows the instructions of the resources' response headers and saves them to the cache. Other client-side caches are warmed up—for example, the DNS cache that saves a map of domain names to IP addresses for resources. Before each test run, however, these caches are flushed to provide a clean and consistent environment.

Throwing out the test client's cache is a great way to simulate the "worst case" scenario in which no resources are locally available, but in reality we know that this is hardly always the case. Users revisit websites all the time and some sites even share resources. For example, the popular jQuery JavaScript library is often included in websites through a shared and public CDN. If a user visits two websites that both reference this resource, the second site will have the performance benefit of using the cached version. So if WebPageTest clears the cache before each test, how can we represent these use cases?

The Repeat View configuration setting is one way that WebPageTest is able to address this (Figure 3-1). To enable it, select the First View and Repeat View option. Each "view" is effectively another instance of the test run. The terminology may be getting confusing at this point, so think of it taxonomically as a single test containing multiple runs, each of which contains one or two views. *First View* refers to the cold cache setup in which nothing is served locally, whereas *Repeat View* refers to the warm cache containing everything instantiated by the first view. In addition to selecting the radio button UI on the page, you can also enable repeat views by setting the query-string parameter fvonly to 0. So, for example, the URL webpagetest.org?fvonly=0 would preset the radio button to the First View and Repeat View option.

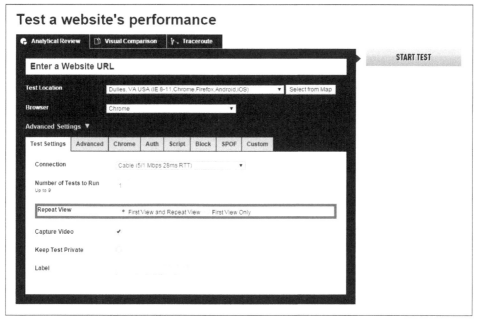

Figure 3-1. The option to enable repeat views for each test run is on the WebPageTest home page in the Advanced Settings section

You may be thinking that you might as well run all tests with this option set. After all, it shows a different perspective that may be useful for analysis. Despite the convenience of always having a repeat view available, keep in mind that someone has to pay for it—not necessarily monetarily but rather with time and resources. You pay for repeat views by waiting for your tests to complete. For all intents and purposes, enabling repeat view effectively doubles the test duration because it executes each test run in both cache states. When you are running many tests or a test with many runs, you can get your results sooner by ensuring that each test does less work. This is also important because WebPageTest is a public tool. It may be the case that there is someone else in the world waiting to run his own test behind yours. The longer your test takes to run, the longer that person has to wait (and the people behind him, too). And it should go without saying, but we will say anyway: WebPageTest itself has finite resources. It's not in danger of running out of space any time soon, but if you could save a few megabytes of disk space by only enabling repeat view when you need it, why not? If you are running your own private instance of WebPageTest, this point may be especially critical. Simply put, use discretion with this and other configuration options that consume additional resources like the number of test runs (which are capped at nine for this reason) and the screenshot/video options.

There are also some limitations to the usefulness of repeat views. By definition, this view is an identical page load to the first view. For the purposes of synthetic testing, this is great for analyzing the cacheability of the resources of a single page. Inconveniently, real users tend to follow a flow of pages—starting at the home page and navigating through to secondary content, for example.

Repeat views are not necessarily able to demonstrate the warm-cache experience that real users experience throughout the website. If a user visits Page B via Page A and you run first and repeat view tests on Page B, you would not be accounting for the differences in resources between the two pages. You may misinterpret the repeat view results to mean that Page B's warm cache state is better than it actually is. The reality is that you need a way to load both pages synthetically in order to represent the scenario of visiting a page with another page's resources in cache. Repeat views are limited to loading a single page with its own resources in cache. To resolve this issue, we will need a more powerful tool that is flexible enough to handle multiple pages. That tool is reserved for a later chapter; see "Flow View" on page 82 for more information.

Analyzing Cachability

After configuring a test to execute repeat views as described in the previous section, you must then analyze the results to determine how well resources are being cached. To do so, you need to know both what to look for and where to look.

How long a resource will be cached by the browser (if at all) is determined by two factors: age and *time to live* (TTL). Both of these values are configured by the server in the form of HTTP headers.

The age of a resource can be identified using one of two headers: *entity tags* (`ETags`) or the `Last-Modified` header. An entity tag is simply a unique identifier representing the content of a resource. As the content changes—for example, updating an image but retaining the same URL—the `ETag` would change respectively. Alternatively, the `Last-Modified` header is a date stamp of the time at which the resource most recently changed, as shown in Example 3-1. Either header can be used to identify the age, or state, of a resource at the time it is downloaded and cached.

Example 3-1. Sample resource age/state HTTP headers

```
Last-Modified: Fri, 19 Jan 2007 04:40:18 GMT
ETag:          W/"0a56eeb833bc71:2f7"
```

After the user's browser has downloaded and cached the resource, it will stay in cache until it is evicted to make room for newer resources, or until it expires. To determine the expiration date, browsers rely on one of two TTL headers: `Expires` or the `max-age` property of `Cache-Control`. The `Expires` header provides a date stamp of the exact moment when the resource will expire. Similarly, the `Cache-Control: max-age` (sometimes referred to as CCMA) header specifies the number of seconds from the time of download until the resource expires. See Example 3-2 for example values for these headers.

Example 3-2. Sample resource TTL HTTP headers

```
Cache-Control: max-age=31536000
Expires:       Fri, 20 Nov 2015 06:50:15 GMT
```

Now that you know what to look for, let's talk about where to find this data. First, you'll need to head over to the results (or details) page for a test run, which is where the waterfall diagrams are shown. Clicking on any request row in the waterfall will invoke a panel with summary information about the resource. The three other tabs in this panel let you drill down into the request headers, response headers, and the response body. From this panel, this chapter is only concerned with the Request and Response tabs.

The Response tab displays all of the headers sent back from the server to the browser, including the caching headers discussed earlier (`ETag`, `Cache-Control`, `Expires`, and `Last-Modified`).

Heuristic Caching

What you see in the repeat-view waterfall diagram is helpful toward understanding which resources must be downloaded across subsequent visits. However, what you don't see may mislead you.

The omission of resources from the repeat-view waterfall suggests that they were served from cache. You would generally be right to assume that these resources were configured to persist across page views, but there are edge cases in which resources may only appear to be correctly configured.

The HTTP/1.1 specification permits user agents to estimate how long to keep a resource in cache using heuristics:

> Since origin servers do not always provide explicit expiration times, HTTP caches typically assign heuristic expiration times, employing algorithms that use other header values (such as the Last-Modified time) to estimate a plausible expiration time. The HTTP/1.1 specification does not provide specific algorithms, but does impose worst-case constraints on their results.

> —13.2.2 Heuristic Expiration, *http://www.w3.org/Protocols/rfc2616/rfc2616-sec13.html*

According to the specification, if a browser downloads a resource with an unknown lifetime, it can assign an expected lifetime known as a *heuristic expiration* time. What this means for you is that the repeat view may not be entirely what it seems. You may incorrectly assume that a resource has been loaded from cache because it has been properly configured to do so. Under some circumstances, a browser may cache a resource even when not explicitly instructed by the server's response headers. As a result, WebPageTest will not show this resource as having loaded over the network in the repeat view waterfall.

You may be wondering why you should even bother to set caching headers in the first place if browsers will do the work for you. The answer is that browsers only estimate how long one of these resources should be cached, and that control should always be in the developer's hands. Despite granting the authority of heuristic expiration to browsers, the specification puts the onus on developers to maintain this control:

> Since heuristic expiration times might compromise semantic transparency, they ought to be used cautiously, and we encourage origin servers to provide explicit expiration times as much as possible.
>
> —13.2.2 Heuristic Expiration, *http://www.w3.org/Protocols/rfc2616/rfc2616-sec13.html*

Furthermore, it's not always clear how long implicitly cached resources should persist. The specification stops short of imposing an algorithm to determine the lifetime of these resources and leaves that up to the browser vendors. One way to get an exact answer is to go directly to the source. That is, check the browser's source code.

Chrome's source code is freely available, so we can see how it implements Section 13.2.2. Of interest is the file for evaluating resources' HTTP response headers, aptly named *http_response_headers.cc*.

```
if ((response_code_ == 200 || response_code_ == 203 ||
     response_code_ == 206) && !must_revalidate) {
  // TODO(darin): Implement a smarter heuristic.
  Time last_modified_value;
  if (GetLastModifiedValue(&last_modified_value)) {
    // The last-modified value can be a date in the future!
    if (last_modified_value <= date_value) {
      lifetimes.freshness = (date_value - last_modified_value) / 10;
      return lifetimes;
    }
  }
}
```

As you can see, a resource can be implicitly cached for up to 10% of the difference between the time it was downloaded and the time it was last modified. In other words, if a user loads a resource only an hour old without any explicit cache headers, Chrome will cache it for six minutes. As the resource ages, its heuristic expiration time also increases. If you consider that the recommended cache lifetime for a static resource is 1 year, realize that you can only get this kind of performance for resources over 10 years old. This is exactly why you should take control of the HTTP response headers to include explicit cache instructions for browsers to ensure that the resource is handled exactly how you intend.

CHAPTER 4

Comparing Tests

By now, you should have a good idea of what to look for when optimizing a page. Supposing you have compressed a few images or delay-loaded a JavaScript file or two, you're probably eager to find out how much of a difference these changes have made. Besides manually loading each individual test's results page side by side, WebPageTest allows you to compare tests with tools especially designed to highlight the differences. In this chapter, we'll look at the comparison tools at your disposal and how WebPageTest makes it all possible.

Perceived Performance

So far we've looked at web performance from a very mechanical point of view. That is to say that we've gathered a lot of great data about how the page is constructed "under the hood," like millisecond-precision event timings. But there's one area of web performance that is arguably more important than simple load-time metrics. That is the measure of how fast a user perceives the page to load: does it *feel* fast? So what's the difference? For example, the user doesn't care if the page-load event fired after one second if the video she was intending to watch doesn't load until five seconds. The literal load time of the page was only one second, but the perceived load time was much longer. Overhyping metrics like the load event can lead us astray when optimizing web pages. We also need to look at performance from the users' perspective and optimize for their experience, which may not necessarily align with WebPageTest's default metrics.

The visual comparison tools described in this chapter address the shortcomings of context-agnostic metrics. These tools are more like a camera than a stopwatch, giving us the ability to actually see the page load just as an end user would. This kind of empathetic analysis allows us to better understand how quick a page feels.

Capture Video

The Capture Video configuration option makes test comparison possible. With this option enabled, screenshots of the page will be taken at regular intervals during loading. These screenshots comprise the filmstrip view and, when shown in succession, make up the video replay. Figure 4-1 shows you where to enable the option.

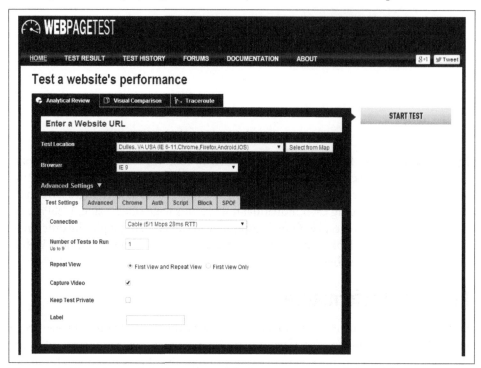

Figure 4-1. The Advanced Settings area of the home page is toggled and the Capture Video checkbox is enabled. This configuration will ensure that screenshots are taken during page load and that test results can be compared against other tests.

To enable this option, select the checkbox on the Test Settings tab of the Advanced Settings section. This tells WebPageTest to save screenshots at regular intervals during the page load process. These still images comprise the frames that will make up a video recording of the loading process. This visual data will form the foundation for the core functionality of the test comparison tool. Only when this configuration is turned on are you able to use the tool to compare against other tests.

There are several querystring parameters that are helpful when you know you're going to be using the test comparison page. On the WebPageTest home page, append these parameters to the URL before starting your test:

- **video=1** ensures that the Capture Video option is always enabled.

- **continuousVideo=1** maintains a consistent frame rate of 10 fps. Without this, the test is not guaranteed to always record screenshots every 100 milliseconds, as it slows down to 1 fps by default.

- **iq=100** alters the image quality of JPEG screenshots to any value between 0 and 100, with 100 being the best quality.

- **pngss=1** formats the final screenshot of the fully loaded page as a PNG image.

Be aware that there are some limitations to the screenshots and the resultant video. First and foremost, screenshots can only be taken of the visible area of the web page, known as the area above the fold. Just like a user's browser window, the test agent's browser has a fixed size outside of which a screenshot is unable to capture. Second, the rate of capture is slow enough to avoid major interference with the CPU. Taking a virtual picture comes at a cost in terms of computation, which must be balanced with the processing required to build the page. For example, if the pictures were taken at a smooth 60 frames per second, the processor would be burdened every 16.7 milliseconds, which could adversely affect test results. For this reason, screenshots are limited to 10 frames per second; fast enough to capture granular changes to the page and slow enough to stay out of the CPU's way. And the last word of caution is related to the quality of the pictures. To save on storage space, screenshots are recorded at lower resolution. The default quality is passable for recognizing prominent elements on the page but unsatisfactory for reading most text.

Filmstrip and Video

In the late nineteenth century, a heated debate had developed over whether a horse in motion was ever completely unsupported midair or if it always had at least one foot on the ground. United States Senator Leland Stanford commissioned Eadweard Muybridge to photograph his galloping horse, Sallie Gardner, to settle the debate scientifically.

Muybridge carefully positioned 24 cameras along a track to capture Stanford's horse in action. As the horse rode by, each camera took a photograph of the horse midstride. What resulted was a set of images all centered on the horse, capturing its movements for further scrutiny. What Muybridge had on film was enough to bury the debate definitively; the horse could be seen momentarily suspended in midair without a foot on the ground. This series of photographs is considered to be one of the first motion pictures ever recorded, known as *Sallie Gardner at a Gallop* or *The Horse in Motion* (Figure 4-2).

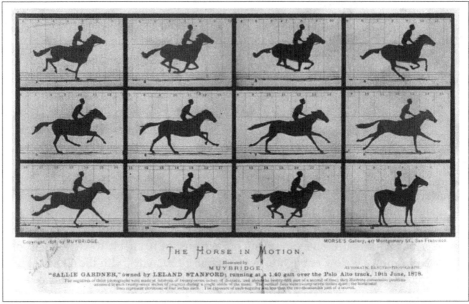

Figure 4-2. Eadweard Muybridge's still photographs of Sallie Gardner in motion

Like the galloping horse, web pages can appear to load too quickly to discern any particular pattern. The naked eye isn't able to break down the process into discrete observable steps, so we use tools to assist us. Muybridge's series of cameras was able to show what the eye couldn't see. WebPageTest's filmstrip is an incredibly powerful tool that similarly captures moments in time, allowing us to better quantify how a page loads visually, as shown in Figure 4-3.

Figure 4-3. Two tests with different connection speed configurations are compared side-by-side visually using the filmstrip view. In this way, it's clear that the top test loads faster.

The Visual Comparison page is only available to tests that have enabled video capture. For these tests, the page is accessible by way of either the test log or the test summary page. The test log lets you refer back to completed tests (Figure 4-4), both those that you started yourself and those that have been set to public by everyone else using the tool. From this page, you are easily able to select multiple tests for comparison. Alternatively, you can see a test's visual progress view from its summary page, as shown in Figure 4-5.

Compare	Date/Time	From	Label	Url
	06/09/14 23:21:33	Dulles, VA - **Chrome - FIOS** (video)	Fiber	http://webpagetest.org
	06/09/14 23:21:27	Dulles, VA - **Chrome - Cable** (video)	Cable	http://webpagetest.org
	06/09/14 23:21:21	Dulles, VA - **Chrome - DSL** (video)	DSL	http://webpagetest.org
	06/09/14 23:21:14	Dulles, VA - **Chrome - Dial** (video)	Dial Up	http://webpagetest.org
	06/09/14 23:21:07	Dulles, VA - **Chrome - 3G** (video)	3G	http://webpagetest.org

View 1 Day ▼ test log for URLs containing | Update List

Show tests from all users   Only list tests that include video   Do not limit the number of results (warning, WILL be slow)

Clicking on an url will bring you to the results for that test

Figure 4-4. Multiple tests are listed, each with its own checkbox to add it to the Visual Comparison page. The Compare button navigates to the page with each selected test's unique ID appended in the URL.

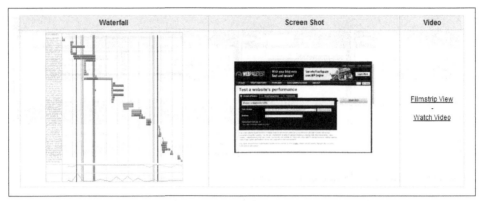

Waterfall	Screen Shot	Video
		Filmstrip View - Watch Video

Figure 4-5. From a test's summary page, the Filmstrip View link on the right takes you to the test's corresponding Visual Comparison page

WebPageTest constructs the filmstrip by taking periodic screenshots of the page above the fold. These images are laid out chronologically so that each passing frame shows the page a little closer to being fully loaded (see Figure 4-6). Like Muybridge's photographs, these still images instill a sense of movement as the page appears to load. Long runs of blank or unchanging images tell you that the page is slow to load. This is exactly the kind of empathetic analysis that makes perceived performance so powerful. Being able to look at test results that evoke a feeling of slowness should make you just as impatient and anxious as a user would feel. Load time is just a number, but seeing a page load is a feeling.

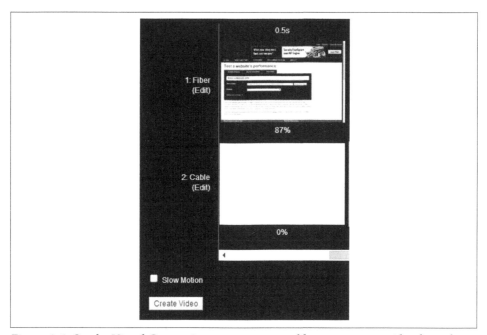

Figure 4-6. On the Visual Comparison page, you are able to generate a video from the selected test filmstrips with the Create Video button. Optionally, the Slow Motion check-box alters the playback speed from 10 fps down to 2 fps, dramatizing each frame of progress.

To truly give you a feeling of the page performance, the filmstrip is second only to the video feature. This is a real-time playback of each frame in the filmstrip. Things get really interesting when you add tests to the comparison; the video will synchronize each test and visualize their progress side by side, as shown in Figure 4-7. This is especially useful for succinctly capturing the difference in performance between tests. To that end, the performance video is great for nontechnical people to see and understand page-load time across tests. A video is easy to watch and doesn't require numbers to complicate the message that one page is faster than another.

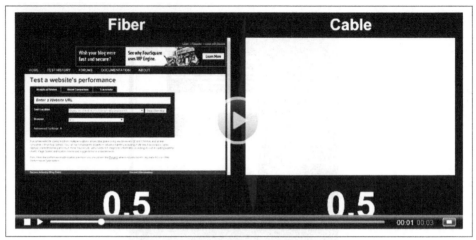

Figure 4-7. The filmstrip comes alive in this real-time video of the WebPageTest home page loading over a fast and slow connection

Storytelling by itself is mentally imaginative. As kids, we would tell stories in an activity called "show and tell," during which everyone would present something they wanted to talk about. Coupled with actually showing something from the story, the activity also becomes visually engaging. In the web performance testing version of "show and tell," the filmstrip and video serve as the tangible parts of the performance story. They can't do it alone, though, so we use these tools in addition to the cold hard metrics and waterfall charts to tell the complete story.

Speed Index

Recall from "Measure What Matters" on page 1 that generic metrics like load time and time-to-first-paint are blind to the context of a page. Unlike the filmstrip and video, which show exactly what is visible to the user at a given time, these cold hard metrics tell you more about how the *page* is doing than how the *user* is doing. WebPageTest invented a new metric to address this specific problem, but it needed to be context-aware like the visual comparison tools. The speed index of a page is derived from each screenshot's visual progress toward being fully loaded (see Figure 4-8). A page that displays more to the user sooner has a lower, or better, speed index than a page that is slower to display content. This property of the speed index is what makes it superior to other metrics; it is a measure of general user experience as it relates to page loading.

To demonstrate the speed index's usefulness, consider two versions of the same page. Both versions paint to the screen and complete loading at exactly the same times. The only difference between them is the rate at which content is painted. Ask any user which version they would prefer and the consensus would always be for a page that shows more content sooner. Even when cold metrics like paint and load time are equal, the user experience begs to differ. The speed index is a measure of this experience.

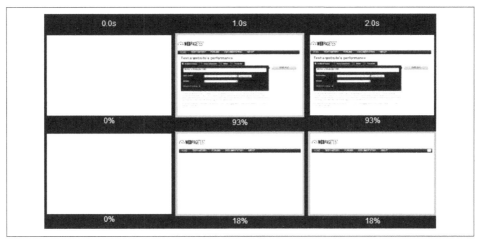

Figure 4-8. Each frame in the filmstrip is annotated with the percentage of the page that has finished loading. This visual progress data forms the basis for the speed index calculation.

When visually comparing these two hypothetical tests, it's clear that one of them appears to load faster. We can graph the visual progress data to illustrate how two versions of the same page could load so differently, as shown in Figure 4-9.

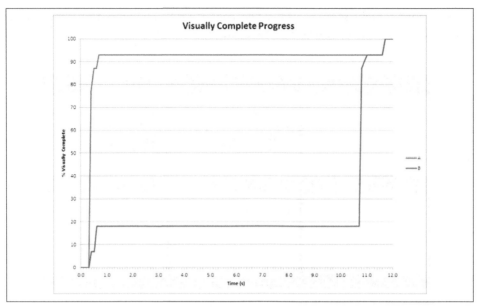

Figure 4-9. The tests' visual progress is plotted in a chart. The test that is perceived to load more quickly climbs higher in visual completeness sooner than the other test, which stagnates below 20% complete for about 10 seconds.

To show how the speed index can be derived from the illustration in Figure 4-9, consider the percentage of content that *is not* rendered at any given time. For the faster test, we can say that there is less to be rendered. Another way of thinking of it is to look at the area above the lines, as shown in Figure 4-10. By shading in these areas, the speed index emerges and the stark difference in area corresponds to small and large indexes.

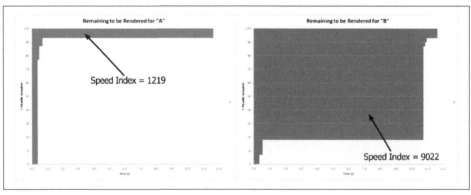

Figure 4-10. The area above each line graph illustrates the amount of content not yet displayed at any given time

Remember that these two tests started and finished displaying content at exactly the same times! But the speed index isn't fooled by a page that takes its time in the middle of the page load. We've seen how it works visually, so how is it computed? In calculus, an integral is used to calculate the area under a curve (see the formula in Figure 4-11). If you're getting anxious flashbacks to math class, don't worry. The integral of the visual progress curve tells us the amount of content that has been displayed, but remember that we're interested in the content yet to be displayed. We can get the area above the curve by subtracting the completed percentage from 1 and integrating the result for each 100-millisecond interval.

 The speed index is much better at representing the quality of a page load's user experience than simpler metrics like first paint and load times. However, it is not a one-size-fits-all number, because it still fails in one important area: application-specific contexts. 100% visual completeness is not necessarily equivalent to total usability of a page. Not only is the page content below the fold excluded from visual measurements, but also WebPageTest has no idea which part of the page users are actually waiting for. For example, a page that is only 25% visually complete may still have enough visible content for a user to start interacting with it. Think of a news page that shows the headline and article immediately but delay-loads other components like the article's corresponding photograph. The story is absolutely readable without the picture; therefore visual completeness is not a perfect indicator of user experience.

$$\text{Speed Index} = \int_0^{end} 1 - \frac{VC}{100}$$

end = end time in milliseconds
VC = % visually complete

Figure 4-11. The speed index formula expressed mathematically, using calculus

Let's see how this is implemented in code:

```
function getSpeedIndex(&$filmstrip) {
    $speed_index = 0;
    $last_time = 0;
    $last_progress = 0;

    foreach($filmstrip['frames'] as $time => &$frame) {
        // The interval between frames.
        $elapsed = $time - $last_time;

        // The area of the rectangle above the current point is length * width,
        // where the length is the remaining progress %
        // and the width is the time interval.
        $speed_index += $elapsed * (100 - $last_progress);

        // Save the current state for the next frame.
        $last_time = $time;
        $last_progress = $frame['progress'];
    }

    return $speed_index;
}
```

Using this relatively straightforward algorithm, we can get a single number that adequately represents the loading performance of a page. The speed index metric is a novel way to look at web performance. You should look at it in your test analysis to give you a more complete idea of performance beyond the default metrics. By doing so, you'll be able to make more-informed decisions about how to better optimize your page.

Summary of Part I

In the preceding chapters, we looked at the basic use cases of WebPageTest. We started by dispelling a couple of common misconceptions about how the tool should be used. WebPageTest is a synthetic tool, which has different applications from RUM. Synthetic tools are excellent for identifying how to make a page faster but not necessarily useful for understanding the actual speeds users are experiencing. The performance metrics that WebPageTest exposes are especially useful for comparison purposes but shouldn't be mistaken for the ground truth of real users' performance.

To understand what could be slowing down a web page, we looked at a few of the tools available in the test analysis report. The flagship tool of WebPageTest is the waterfall diagram. Having discussed each constituent part of a waterfall, we came to a better understanding of what to expect from it. For example, the shape of a waterfall says a lot about the underlying performance of the page. A waterfall's shape can be broken down further into discrete slopes of horizontal and vertical imaginary lines that indicate which requests are contributing to poor performance. We also looked at the connection view, which is just a different way of visualizing the network activity, the difference being that requests are grouped by the channel over which they are served.

Using the waterfall and connection views, we were able to come up with a list of anti-patterns in which bad performance manifests itself. Of the anti-patterns to look out for, the most common and severe is the long first-byte time. When the initial request takes a long time to process, the entire page is delayed and literally nothing can proceed. Ironically, WebPageTest is not well-equipped for us to figure out exactly why the response was delayed. Additional tools are required to trace the source of the problem. WebPageTest is, by design, a client-side analysis tool—one of many tools you should keep at your disposal when testing web performance.

In addition to the network visualizations, we also studied the way that WebPageTest grades tests. These grades are meant to be the most essential performance optimizations that should be universally applicable to all pages. For example, images are the most ubiquitous resource type on the web and yet they are too often transferred with unnecessary bloat. The Compress Images grade analyzes a test's images to see just how much could have been saved with basic image compression techniques. The greater the savings, the worse of a grade the test will receive. Unlike the raw data, these grades try to do some of the analysis for you by calling out the more egregious categories of inefficiencies.

And finally, we saw how to compare tests so that the differences between them become more apparent. The clearest way to show how two tests differ is to look at them visually by making use of the filmstrip and video tools. The filmstrip view shows screenshots at periodic intervals, allowing us to see exactly what is visible on screen. These screenshots are postprocessed so that we're able to determine their visual completeness, or the percentage of the page that has completed loading. This metric gives way to the speed index metric, which is a radically different way of measuring page performance. We talked about how perceived performance is in tune with how users perceive a page load. The perception of performance can be totally unlike the "cold" performance metrics that serve (for the most part) to report on distinct browser events like when the DOM is ready or when the page has loaded. The speed index quantifies the user experience based on the rate at which a page loads. Loading more content to the screen sooner just *feels* faster to the user. Of course, this is only as useful as the relevance of the content being displayed. That's why the filmstrip and video tools are so important, because we're able to see exactly which parts of the page are rendering and when.

These basic use cases have formed a solid foundation upon which we will build up a more thorough understanding of how to use WebPageTest like the experts. For most people, this may be enough to get started and make impactful web performance optimizations. If you're someone who needs to get more out of WebPageTest, continue reading to learn about how to use its more advanced features.

PART II

Intermediate Use Cases

Most of Part I was concerned with understanding how to analyze WebPageTest results. Having completed Part I, you should now be comfortable reading waterfall diagrams, comparing tests, and getting down to business determining what is slowing down your page. These skills are extremely valuable and will only get sharper as we continue looking at the next level of use cases.

Up until now, however, our test configurations have been overly simplified. As you've seen, WebPageTest makes it very easy to get results for a particular URL. With few exceptions, the test settings we've looked at so far have been left at their default values. As easy as it is to leave these settings untouched, the test results can lose relevance and usefulness if the test is misconfigured.

In Part II, we will build on the foundation of test analysis by discussing the use cases of test configuration. For each of the following chapters, a unique use case will be examined. We'll discuss ways to use WebPageTest's flexible configuration options to address each scenario, providing you with the skills you need to adequately test your website.

CHAPTER 5

Simulating Real Users

In Part I, the first thing we said about WebPageTest was that it is a synthetic tool, not to be confused with real-user monitoring. By virtue of being synthetic, WebPageTest is only an approximation of page loading performance. But synthetic testing can (and should!) still accurately resemble the way actual users access the page.

Why would it matter if a synthetic test is realistic? It is completely within the realm of possibility that a user with an empty browser cache from Dulles, Virginia in Internet Explorer 9 over a cable Internet connection is visiting a given web page. The goal of synthetic testing, however, is not necessarily to optimize for one particular use case but rather to optimize for the entire user base. The best way to do that is to set up synthetic tests that are representative of the population. For example, test in a commonly used browser from a typical location over reasonable network speeds. These simple changes allow you to focus on the performance issues that actually matter to users.

To make the point, imagine that you're contracted to optimize the performance of a university web page for enrolled students to check their class schedules. You can assume that users are likely to be on very fast university infrastructure, and there's a good chance that they will be accessing the site from their mobile phones as they figure out when and where their next class is. Given this information, a good test configuration would make use of a mobile browser with a fast connection in a location geographically proximate to the university. By establishing the synthetic test in a way that simulates a student accessing the page, you're better able to identify performance issues that are actually affecting real users.

This scenario, though contrived, demonstrates the importance of simulating real users. If you only test with the WebPageTest defaults, you might overlook issues specific to mobile usage. What if the hypothetical university happens to be located in London, England? That would be a useful piece of information to have so that you could choose one of WebPageTest's London test agents. Testing geographically close to the servers would mean that the browser and server have a shorter path over which to communicate, leading to faster round-trip times or latency. Carelessly testing from the default location in Dulles, Virginia would include unrealistic traces of transatlantic latency in the results. The last thing you want to do is spend time fixing a problem that doesn't even exist, so avoid polluting test results with costly distractions.

 When a user revisits a page configured to cache its resources, the browser is able to make use of the local copy and avoid downloading the resources all over again. This is great for performance because, as the saying goes, the fastest network request is the one you never even have to make. The cache state is such an important factor precisely because it's so impactful. A page loaded with a warm cache is usually much faster than its cold counterpart. If users typically hit a page with a warm cache, overanalyzing WebPageTest's first-view results is less likely to lead to meaningful insights.

WebPageTest's configurability makes real-user simulation possible. As we saw in the university example, we could select test parameters, such as mobile device, connection speed, and test location, to ensure realism. The configuration options extend to the application layer as well, which means that WebPageTest can actually initialize tests by interacting with the web page itself. A significant issue we haven't considered yet is user authentication. The fact that the application shows a student his own personalized schedule must mean that it knows who that student is. So how can WebPageTest tell the application whose schedule to use? As we'll see in detail in Chapter 9, there are a few techniques to give WebPageTest access to privileged user data and simulate signing in. For the purposes of this chapter, you should just be aware that these capabilities exist.

Identifying Demographics

In the previous example of the university course schedule page, you were given several pieces of information about the users. Knowing that the users are students, accessing the page from their mobile devices, on campus, and connected to university WiFi, you are better able to simulate their experience in a synthetic test. Understanding who is actually using a website is as vital as understanding how they access it. For our hypothetical scenario, that all sounds great. But reality is never so simple.

The process of understanding your users could take several low- or high-tech routes. One of the easiest and most direct ways would be to post a survey for your users. Think of a web form that users fill out to provide you with their personal information. Potential questions could be, "Where are you?" or "What browser/device are you using?" This virtual census relies on users to volunteer their information to you, which you must then save and organize into meaningful metrics. While these results would be accurate and custom-tailored to the questions you're specifically looking to answer, users generally don't want to be bothered with online surveys, especially when it comes to personal information. This method also gets in the way of what the users came to your website to do, and could lead to negative behavior like an increased bounce rate. For these reasons, it's probably not a good idea to take the low-tech approach.

Fortunately, several high-tech options are available in the form of real-user monitoring. Although RUM has been discussed so far primarily as a web performance tool, it is also suitable for surveying real-user demographics. You may be wondering how this can be done without users volunteering their information such as by entering their browser and location into a web form. The good news is that much of this data can be inferred from the communications already going on between the user's browser and the web server. Browsers use HTTP request headers to include not only information about the resource they want but also information about themselves. For example, a Chrome browser would include the `User Agent` request header with a value similar to `Mozilla/5.0 (Windows NT 6.1; WOW64) AppleWebKit/537.36 (KHTML, like Gecko) Chrome/36.0.1985.125 Safari/537.36`. Additionally, the server already knows the user's IP address, which is necessary to be able to route responses back to the user. The user agent header and IP address can be used to infer the user's browser, operating system, and coarse geographical location.

In addition to user metrics, RUM services are also well-equipped to collect page data. Another HTTP request header is `Referer`, which is intentionally misspelled to maintain consistency with the HTTP specification. This header denotes the URL of the page that the user was on when the request was made. By linking user data like IP address with page data, the services are able to interpolate patterns such as navigation flow through a website. RUM services are also capable of handling application-specific data. For example, a website may have content that makes use of a Flash player. Because not everyone has the Flash plug-in installed, it would be useful for the service to include the proportion of clients that can support Flash.

All of this is made possible by the web page including a callback to the RUM service. The callback is made in the form of an HTTP request to the RUM API endpoint. In addition to the data captured by the HTTP request headers (IP address, `User-Agent`, `Referer`), the web page could also attach application data just like a form would turn input fields into request data on submit. By making this request from the user's browser on the web page directly to the RUM service, all of the aforementioned metrics become available to the service to store and analyze.

Adding a RUM service to your website gives you the ability to not only monitor performance but also capture valuable information about who your users are. And because RUM constantly ingests live data, you can see how users change the way they access your site over time. For the purposes of configuring synthetic tests, there is no better source of truth than RUM data. There are many great RUM services available like Google Analytics (Figure 5-1) and SOASTA mPulse. These tools all have several core features in common like web performance monitoring and reporting of user geography and technology. But because Google Analytics is the most prominent RUM tool in use on the web, we'll use that to demonstrate how to identify user demographics in live user data. Translating these instructions to other RUM tools or even newer versions of Google Analytics should be straightforward given the similarity between features.

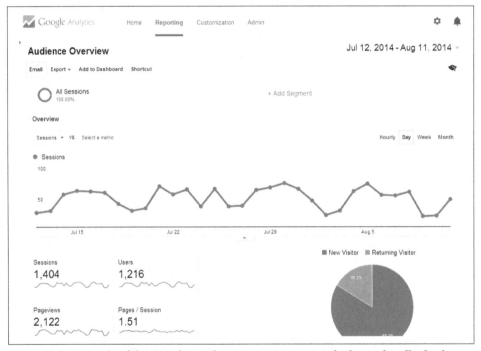

Figure 5-1. Example of the Google Analytics overview page, which graphically displays information about website traffic over a given period of time

Each of the following sections will look at a demographic, walk you through identifying it in Google Analytics, and demonstrate how to configure it on WebPageTest. The sections will increase in complexity, starting with the most-viewed pages of a site. The following three sections will take you through the browser/device, location, and connection-speed user metrics.

Popular Pages

Suffice it to say that the pages that you test on WebPageTest should generally be pages that your users frequently visit. This application metric is the most straightforward for RUM services to analyze because it is just a count of the distinct HTTP `Referer` values. On Google Analytics, you can find your popular pages by navigating to the All Pages table under Behavior > Site Content. Figure 5-2 shows the most popular pages for an example website.

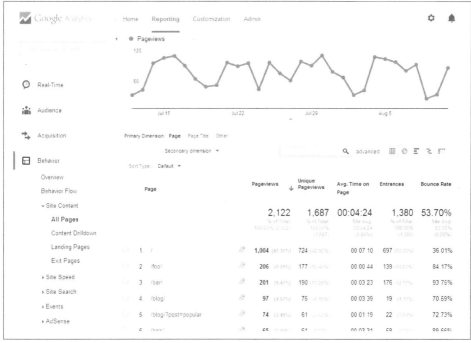

Figure 5-2. Table of fictional web pages for the website www.example.com, sorted by page views. The home page (/) is the most popular page.

Figure 5-2 shows us that the home page accounts for almost half of all page views, so that would definitely qualify as a good URL to run on WebPageTest. */foo/* and */bar/* are the next two most-popular pages, so for more complete coverage it would be a good idea to add test cases for these URLs on WebPageTest as well (Figure 5-3).

The list of popular pages is not grouped. This means that if your page varies by querystring data, each unique URL would be counted separately. The example website used in Figure 5-2 contains a blog. Each blog post can be directly accessed with the `?post=[title]` querystring parameter. When all blog posts are considered, it's possible that in aggregate the blog is the most popular page of the entire site. Because Google Analytics breaks down pages by unique URL, you are only able to see which blog posts are individually the most popular. The popularity of the blog as a single page type, like the home page or secondary pages like */foo/* and */bar/*, is not directly comparable. The current implementation means that you would only be able to determine the relative popularity of individual blog posts instead. This may become an issue if you have many individual pages that each contribute many page views, but not as many as other more popular standalone pages. When you look at a list of pages sorted by page view, you may make the mistake of ignoring the other ungrouped pages.

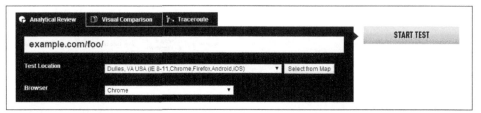

Figure 5-3. One of the most popular page URLs as determined by Google Analytics is fed into WebPageTest via the URL text input field on the test configuration home page

When you select pages to use for testing, popularity should not be the only factor. You must also consider pages on which performance is a business-critical requirement. For example, an ecommerce web site may want to audit the performance of the product pages or the checkout flow. These pages may not show up in the analytics report as some of the most frequented pages on the entire site, but that should not diminish the importance of page-loading performance, due to their direct business impact.

Device and Browser

Up until 2007, the year of the first iPhone, it would be uncommon to see web traffic from anything but desktop computers. But the web-enabled mobile device revolution has now made it possible for users to access web pages from their phones. Google Analytics can show you the breakdown of traffic from traditional desktop, mobile (phone), and tablet devices, as shown in Figure 5-4.

Figure 5-4. The Mobile Overview page breaks down website traffic by the type of device used: desktop computer, mobile phone, and tablet. In this screenshot, desktop overshadows mobile and tablet traffic at 93.5%, with mobile following at 4.5%, and tablet taking up the remaining 2%. This lack of device diversity would suggest that desktop-only testing would be sufficient.

The mobile overview page, as shown in Figure 5-4, is accessible from the Mobile section under the Audience heading. The interesting part of this page is the device category breakdown, which in this case shows desktop commanding over 90% of traffic. Depending on the type of website being analyzed, mobile could easily overtake desktop traffic. If your website is frequently visited by mobile users, you should be pleased to know that as of February 2014, WebPageTest has been upgraded to an arsenal of mobile devices for your testing needs. Figure 5-5 shows you how to select a testing location from the WebPageTest home page.

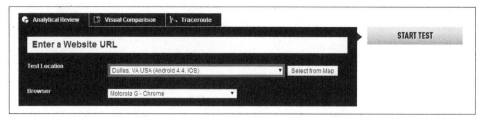

Figure 5-5. On the WebPageTest home page, selecting the test location in Dulles, Virginia gives you access to a variety of actual mobile devices on which to test

The list of test locations on the WebPageTest home page includes a section just for mobile devices in Dulles, Virginia. This location is equipped with an iPhone 4 as well as several Android 4.4 devices including the Motorola E, Motorola G, Nexus 5, and Nexus 7 tablet.

In addition to the device category, the type of browser used is also relevant. This information can also be found on the Technology tab under the Audience heading. The Browser & OS page defaults to showing you a list of the most popular browsers, as shown in Figure 5-6.

Figure 5-6. The Browser & OS page defaults to a list of the website's most popular browsers. In this screenshot, Chrome makes up 64%, Firefox 20%, Safari 10%, Internet Explorer trailing at about 4%, and other miscellaneous browsers comprising the rest. Based on this data, you might choose to test in both Chrome and Firefox on WebPageTest.

The data shown in Figure 5-6 indicates that the Chrome browser accounts for almost two-thirds of traffic. If this were your website being analyzed, this should be a signal to you that your test configuration should focus on this particular browser. But does this mean that Chrome is also the most popular browser on mobile devices? We know that phones and tables are able to support a variety of browsers. To get a breakdown of mobile browser traffic, you can modify any page to narrow the traffic to only the mobile segment of users, as shown in Figure 5-7.

Figure 5-7. This screenshot shows how to segment traffic by mobile and tablet devices. This was accomplished by changing the All Sessions segment, which represents 100% of traffic, to the Mobile and Tablet Traffic segment, which is only 6.5% of the total. Doing this on the Browser & OS page allows you to view the website's most popular mobile browsers and operating systems.

As the title of the page suggests, the Browser & OS page also allows you to view a breakdown of device operating systems. This is especially useful when you are viewing the mobile segment of traffic. Switching to view the list of most popular operating systems can be done by changing the primary dimension, the control for which can be found above the data table.

Although this provides a more realistic view into actual mobile usage, WebPageTest is only able to provide basic browser support for testing on mobile devices such as Chrome on Android and Safari on iOS. Mobile browsers, such as the native Android Browser, Opera Mini, and Firefox, are unfortunately not supported as of the time of writing.

Geographic Location

The location from where your tests are run matters. Lack of attention to this usually comes in two forms: testing unrealistically close to or far from the server. For example, a private test agent could be set up on the same physical network as the web server itself. This is akin to running a web server on your laptop and testing the page-load performance by opening a browser on the same machine. The time for the test agent to communicate with the server is so small that no live user could ever experience it. Conversely, it's even easier to configure a test to run unrealistically far from the server. Imagine an Australian-based website being tested from the default WebPageTest agent in the US. If the majority of traffic originates from the US, this might make sense. However, if the website primarily serves Australians, then the latency overhead just to make one round-trip would be quixotically distracting from the actual performance issues.

As noted in *High Performance Browser Networking* (O'Reilly) by Ilya Grigorik, "the performance of most web applications is limited by latency, not bandwidth, and while bandwidth speeds will continue to increase, unfortunately the same can't be said for latency." When it comes to configuring WebPageTest, geographic location is becoming even more important considering its direct impact on the latency performance bottleneck. Due to the number of round-trips needed to service a request, latency is actually the limiting factor, not bandwidth. It is for this reason that understanding real-user demographics like geographic location are so critical. Figure 5-8 shows us a view of Google Analytics' visitor geolocation page.

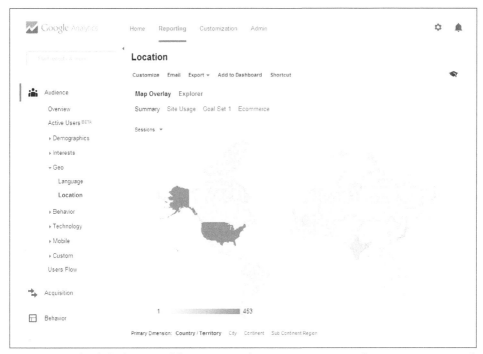

Figure 5-8. The default view of the visitor geolocation page. Visitor locations are grouped by country.

In order to determine where users are from, we turn to Google Analytics' Audience category, under the Geo heading. This provides a map view of recent visitors, grouped by country by default. It turns out, though, that population-dense countries like India may actually be skewing the results. Popular areas that span multiple countries, like regions of Europe, are underrepresented in this kind of visualization. To account for this, Google Analytics also groups visitors by subcontinent regions (as shown in Figure 5-9). For example, France and Germany are in Western Europe, while countries like Mexico and Honduras are considered Central America. These regions provide a level of detail coarse enough to account for congested political boundaries while still accurately conveying areas of interest.

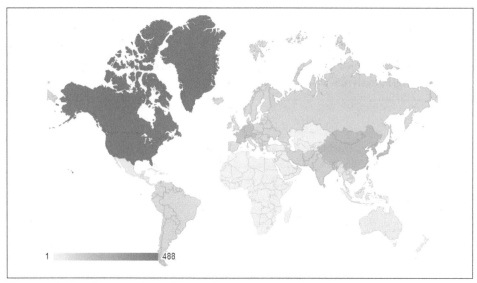

Figure 5-9. An alternate view of visitor locations groups by subcontinent region

The table in Figure 5-10 suggests that to account for at least 50% of visitors, tests should be run from North America, Eastern Asia, and Western Europe.

	Acquisition		
Sub Continent Region	Sessions ↓	% New Sessions	New Users
	1,474 % of Total: 100.00% (1,474)	**83.58%** Site Avg: 83.58% (0.00%)	**1,232** % of Total: 100.00% (1,232)
1. Northern America	**488** (33.11%)	85.04%	415 (33.69%)
2. Eastern Asia	**183** (12.42%)	75.41%	138 (11.20%)
3. Western Europe	**176** (11.94%)	75.00%	132 (10.71%)

Figure 5-10. Western Europe as a whole accounts for more traffic than just India. In country view, however, India overshadows all other European countries individually.

We can drill down into these regions to see the geographic distribution of traffic within the region. On this particular website, North American traffic overwhelmingly originates from the US. Within the US, only a few states account for most of the traffic: California, New York, and Virginia. WebPageTest may not always have a test agent available in the particular region that accounts for the majority of traffic on your own website, but a neighboring test agent is the next best thing.

Figure 5-11 shows the test agent locations all around the world. This map can be used to select an agent geographically close to regions in which traffic is highest.

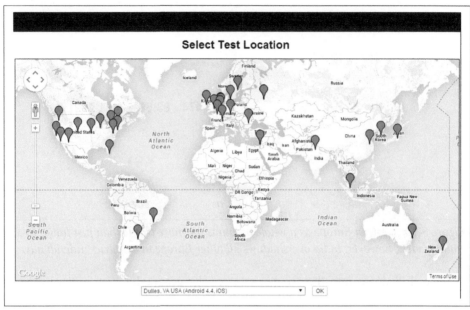

Figure 5-11. WebPageTest visualizes test agent locations on a map. Pins are placed around the world to illustrate the presence of a WebPageTest-enabled machine available for use.

Connection Speed

If you've ever connected to the Internet over a dial-up modem, you know how frustratingly slow web pages can be. Modern hardware has advanced well beyond dial-up; now we have fiber optic connections near the speed of light. The Web itself has also taken on a different shape. As a whole, the Web has gotten heavier, rich with high-resolution images and video. Users can now take advantage of higher speeds by streaming video from services like YouTube and Netflix, which accounts for about half of North America's Internet traffic. Unfortunately, not everyone has the privilege of access to high-speed Internet. These users experience the Web much more slowly. In the spirit of this chapter to synthesize tests that represent the actual user experience, controlling test connection speed is equally important.

Real users' connection speeds are not explicitly tracked in RUM. By using some of the metrics we've already explored (and some trial and error) we can make a good approximation. Let's start by looking at the page-load times for our example website (Figure 5-12).

Figure 5-12. By default, the Page Timings view shows the average page-load time for the entire site over time

You can view the average page-load time for any given page, so let's start by narrowing down to the most popular page. In Figure 5-2, we observed that the home page accounts for about 40% of all traffic. Click on the home page URL in the table below the chart to filter the page speed results to only this page.

Also recall from the previous section that geography plays an important role in web performance, so we will use the table from Figure 5-10 to select the North American subcontinent region (Figure 5-13).

Figure 5-13. Looking at the page-load times per subcontinent region, it's easier to see the difference in load time across the world. This view also allows us to drill down to specific regions.

To get a more accurate idea of typical page-load time, we need to look at the median time as opposed to the average by default. Statistically, the median (or 50th percentile) of a data set represents the middlemost value, which is unaffected by however large or small the outliers may be. Averages take outliers into account and can be misleading when interpreted by themselves. Switching from Map Overlay to the Distribution view produces a much better look at a histogram of load times (Figure 5-14). Using this, we can deduce the median load-time range by finding the load time at which it accounts for 50% of the total.

Figure 5-14. We can drill down the page-load time buckets to half-second increments to calculate the range in which the 50th percentile of users exist

To read this chart, start with the percentage of the first bucket, 0–1 second, which is about 28%. This is less than 50%, so we look at the next bucket, which accounts for another 58%. This exceeds the median value, so we can drill down to get finer bucket values. At 1–1.5 seconds, an additional 14% is accounted for, bringing the total to 42%. The 1.5–2 second bucket adds another 17%, so we know the 50th percentile lies in this range.

Now comes the trial and error. On WebPageTest, create a few tests of the same page originating from the same subcontinent region, in this case somewhere in North America. In each test, choose a different connection-speed profile: dial-up, DSL, cable, or fiber. What we're looking for is a connection that produces results with a load time somewhere in the 1.5–second range. Let's say that cable came the closest at 2.2 seconds. We can speed this up to fall in that Goldilocks range by customizing the connection speed, as shown in Figure 5-15.

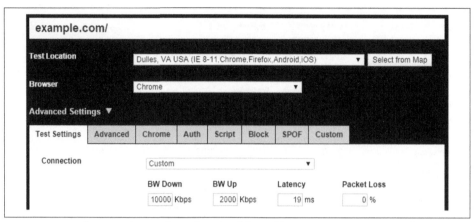

Figure 5-15. Adjusting the up/down bandwidth and latency settings gives us finer control over the speed resources travel over the network

The techniques discussed in this chapter enable you to set up your synthetic tests in a way that reflects typical usage. By leveraging software that aggregates real-user demographics, you're able to determine the most accurate settings to represent your visitors.

With the assurance that your tests are accurate representations of live traffic, scrutiny of performance issues that manifest themselves in synthetic test results carries more weight. Optimizing the synthetic experience will more likely translate to an optimized real-user experience when you're able to focus on the issues that actually affect them.

CHAPTER 6

Mobile Testing

Generally speaking, traditional web developers have always had to ensure that their code worked across popular browsers. This has become the universal truth of web development; users can and will access the web however they are able. In recent years, the freedom of accessibility has become less about "taking back the Web" by choice of browser and more about convenience of access with mobile devices. And it hasn't stopped at mobile phones, either. People will access the web on their tablets and watches, and they will even get it projected onto their eyeball if they so desire. While we're still waiting for the wearable WebPageTest agent, there is already support for tablets and phones.

In this chapter, we will explore the options that WebPageTest provides for mobile web performance testing. Mobile support falls under two categories: emulation and native. Rather than testing on an actual phone or tablet, emulation runs on desktop browsers configured to act like a mobile device. For the real thing, WebPageTest agents can actually control physical mobile devices. As we'll discuss, each tool has its drawbacks and advantages.

Desktop Emulation

It is common for web developers to call their site "mobile-friendly" if it is responsive. One way to do this is to give mobile devices the entire desktop page and rely on client-side code to force it to be mobile-friendly. For example, a page could be viewed on a large desktop monitor or a small phone screen, and some savvy CSS rules could keep everything fitting like a glove. The CSS can work on large or small screen sizes by using media queries to adjust the styles that are applied to the page based on the dimensions of the screen. For a desktop browser to fool a media query, all it has to do is change its viewport size to be as small as a mobile device.

One obvious problem with this approach is that the mobile client must download all of the code required for the desktop view, which may not entirely be used in the mobile view. As we'll discuss more in "Traffic Shaping" on page 77, unnecessary content can have a profound impact on performance as a result of limited download capacity. Many web developers have recognized this problem and have come up with another way to serve mobile web content. The User-Agent property included in the browser's request headers provides the server with demographic information about the user's device. Servers can tell whether the user is on a desktop or mobile device based on the information in this header. So instead of relying on client-side code like CSS to adjust the page layout from desktop to mobile-friendly, the server will use the User-Agent header to provide trimmed-down mobile code whenever necessary. Tricking a server into giving a desktop browser its mobile web page can easily be done by modifying the browser's User-Agent value.

WebPageTest can create a desktop browser with a small viewport as well as overwrite its User-Agent identity. This is the basis for mobile web-browser emulation with desktop browsers. Let's look at how to enable these options.

Any test location that supports Chrome can emulate a mobile device. To configure this, go to the Chrome tab of the Advanced Settings section. Check the Emulate Mobile Device option, as shown in Figure 6-1, and start the test. That's it.

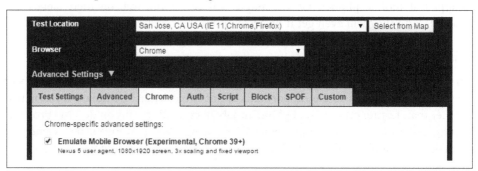

Figure 6-1. The option to enable mobile emulation is found on the Chrome tab of the Advanced Settings section. This will cause desktop Chrome to masquerade as a Nexus 5 and compel the server to produce the mobile web version of the test page.

As a result, the browser will identify itself as something like "Mozilla/5.0 (Linux; Android 4.4.4; Nexus 5 Build/KTU84P) AppleWebKit/537.36 (KHTML like Gecko) Chrome/37.0.2062.55 Mobile Safari/537.36," which is a Nexus 5 device running Chrome 37. It will also adjust the viewport to match the Nexus 5 with a 1080 x 1920 px screen and 3x pixel density.

You can specify your own User-Agent value on the same tab that allows you to enable mobile device emulation. It's also possible to configure the browser window to be as small as a mobile device by programmatically adjusting the viewport size with a scripting command. For example, in the Script tab, you would enter setViewport Size 1080 1920 to achieve the same viewport as a Nexus 5; 1080 pixels wide and 1920 pixels tall. These two options give you the flexibility to emulate any device configuration. See Chapter 7 for a more thorough introduction to using the Script tab.

The test results for an emulated mobile web page appear just like those for a desktop page. You still get the waterfall diagram, screenshots, video of the loading progress, and detailed analysis. However, emulation does come with shortcomings. Desktop computers generally have more powerful CPUs that can build a web page faster than a mobile device. Desktops also have the capacity for much larger browser caches, which means that repeat views may be uncharacteristically optimistic under emulation. Perhaps the most significant factor is the connection speed, which can be drastically slower on a mobile network.

Despite these limitations, there is still something to be learned from emulation. Especially when mobile tests are compared against straightforward desktop tests, egregious "mobile-unfriendly" anti-patterns can be spotted. Look at the size of static resources, for example. Just by counting the bytes, you can tell if a mobile site is unoptimized if the sizes are all equal (Figure 6-2 and Figure 6-3). Alternatively, you could see whether the size of one type of resource is disproportionately high.

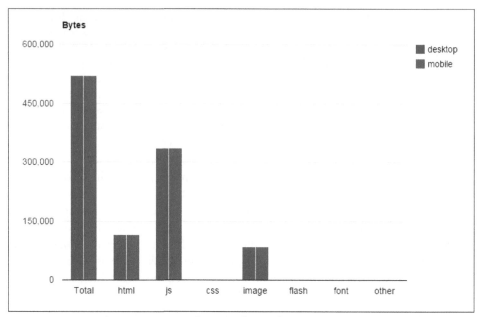

Figure 6-2. Using the A/B testing techniques from Chapter 3, we can use the automatically generated charts to compare the resources of multiple tests. Here, we compare resources of a desktop page against its unoptimized mobile counterpart. The total number of bytes loaded for markup, scripts, styles, and images are all identical. This is a red flag that the mobile page has hardly been optimized—if at all.

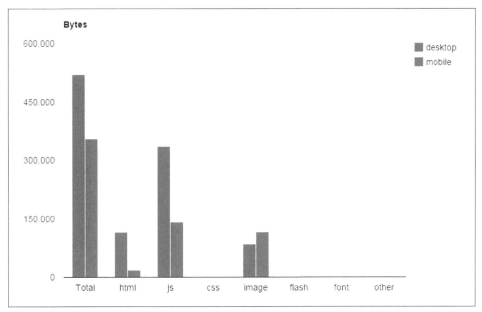

Figure 6-3. Even after some optimizations have been made to the mobile web page, this chart can show us when mobile is loading more of something than desktop. In this case the mobile page has more image bytes. Considering that the screen size is much smaller and the design is much simpler, this should be an automatic red flag to warn against wastefully loading images that are larger than necessary.

WebPageTest can account for the blind spots of emulation with additional tooling. The following sections each address a particular blind spot: simulating the connection speeds commonly experienced on mobile devices, and getting accurate results by testing on physical devices.

Traffic Shaping

In order to simulate a mobile web page in a desktop browser, we need to use Chrome's emulation mode. This encourages the web server to give the browser the mobile version of the page, but the browser still has many properties that are unlike a mobile experience. As most mobile users would be quick to point out, the connection speed on a mobile device is typically much worse than on a desktop connection. WebPageTest accommodates this discrepancy by changing the way the desktop test agent is able to communicate over the network. This technique, called *traffic shaping*, allows test agents to simulate slow connection speeds.

We looked at traffic shaping in "Connection Speed" on page 68 to find a speed that is representative of the real-user population. Instead of varying the connection speed to find realistic results with trial and error, we already know the network type that we're looking for. For the purpose of emulating a mobile device, we can simulate the network conditions by choosing one of the preconfigured mobile profiles, as shown in Figure 6-4.

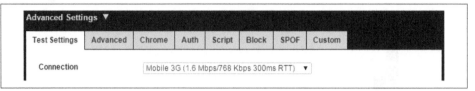

Figure 6-4. You can select one of WebPageTest's preconfigured connection profiles on the Test Settings tab of Advanced Settings. You could also configure a custom connection profile by supplying your own download speed, upload speed, and round-trip time (RTT).

WebPageTest offers two mobile profiles for throttling the test agent's network speed: 3G and Fast 3G. Both profiles share the same upload and download speeds of 1.6 and 0.768 Mbps respectively. The difference is that the 3G profile's RTT is half as fast as Fast 3G's. Keep in mind that the TCP handshake alone is one full round trip, so just opening up a single connection on the slower 3G profile takes a minimum of 300 ms as opposed to 150 ms on Fast 3G.

Modern cellular networks utilize faster technologies like 4G. Even though this option is not explicitly preconfigured in WebPageTest, you can still represent this demographic by choosing the Custom connection and specifying comparable download, upload, and RTT values. For 4G, one approximation would be to configure 5 and 2 Mbps for download and upload speeds respectively, and 75 ms for RTT. These values came from researching typical speeds and may vary depending on location and carrier.

Native Devices

So far, our mobile tests have been configured to run in a desktop browser. The browser disguises itself as a mobile user agent and shrinks its viewport to handheld proportions. The WebPageTest test agent throttles the connection to be more realistic to cellular network performance. The shortcoming of desktop emulation is that the hardware powering the browser is still that of a desktop. What we need is a way to run synthetic performance tests on real mobile devices.

The difference that native hardware offers to synthetic testing is in the computation power. Even when you load identical web pages over identical connection speeds, a mobile device will generally take longer to load than a desktop browser. This is because of the underlying hardware that does the heavy lifting of building the page to display on screen. Mobile devices are smaller by nature and hence they have less room for hardware. This forces a trade-off between size and performance: a smaller

CPU can fit in a phone but is not as powerful, whereas a desktop CPU can take up as much space as it needs. Memory is also a significant factor. The browser cache on a mobile phone can be as little as 5% of that of its desktop counterpart. This introduces another common computational trade-off between the speed of a program and the amount of space it can take up. The relationship between speed and space means that (all other things being equal) a smaller cache would mean a slower running time. For mobile synthetic testing, these factors directly affect metrics like the load time of a page because the phone or tablet is slower by design.

Recall from "Device and Browser" on page 60 that WebPageTest has native iOS and Android devices available for public use. Running tests for these devices is just as easy as any other configuration. To start, choose a geographic location with one of these devices on site, and then pick your device, as shown in Figure 6-5.

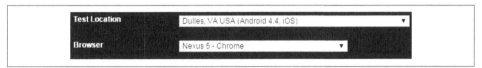

Figure 6-5. Testing on a native device is as straightforward as selecting a mobile-supported location and picking your device

Note, however, that the availability of mobile devices is extremely limited. Only about a dozen devices are available and they are all located in Dulles, Virginia, maintained personally by WebPageTest's creator (Figure 6-6). Keep this in mind when running your mobile tests. Most important, consider the queue of people who may want to use these scarcely available resources and keep tests to a minimum. You should also consider the effects of the devices' location. There will be latency inherent to the physical location of the test agents, especially if they are testing a web page served oceans away.

Figure 6-6. In this 2014 photo, the actual Android devices hooked up to the WebPageTest agent in Dulles, Virginia are shown. From left to right: Nexus 7 (landscape), Nexus 7 (portrait), two Nexus 5, five Motorola G, and two Motorola E. Source: Android web performance testing takes a big leap forward (http://blog.patrickmeenan.com/2014/02/android-web-performance-testing-takes.html)

These publicly available mobile devices do not communicate over a cellular network. They are connected to a traffic-shaped WiFi network, which is deliberately done for reliability. In order to keep the mobile test agents online and unaffected by capricious network conditions, they are relegated to a 3G-shaped traffic configuration. This connection speed is preset for you, as it is the only option compatible with the native mobile devices.

If traffic shaping does not suit your needs and your tests require native mobile devices on their native cellular networks, WebPageTest can still work for you. With a private instance of WebPageTest, you can create your own mobile test agent by installing testing software on a native device. See "Mobile Test Agents" on page 143 for more information about setting this up.

CHAPTER 7

Scripting Preconditions

Chapters 5 and 6 focused on different ways to configure WebPageTest to more accurately represent how real users access a page. We considered the browser, connection speed, geographic location, and device type as customizable options. One thing that has been relatively unmentioned so far is the state of the page and how that can have an effect on its performance.

The cache state of a page has been discussed earlier, but as noted in "Enabling Repeat View" on page 32, we cannot simply rely on the repeat view to represent the cache state of a page. This view is useful for illustrating the resources that could benefit from client-side persistence through the narrow perspective of reloading a page to see what still needs to be downloaded. Realistically, however, users don't just visit a page and reload it. There are other vectors in which a page could be warmed up with the user's prior browsing history.

Two examples of this would be caching of resources both internal and external to the site. Resources can be shared between pages of the same site, such as a common stylesheet or masthead logo. Going from one page to another doesn't usually require that these resources be downloaded again. External resources can also be shared between pages on different sites. Third-party resources like CDN-hosted JavaScript libraries may already be cached on a user's machine before the user ever visits a page that requires that resource. When the user visits such a page for the first time, this is one fewer resource that needs to be downloaded. In both of these examples, the page is in an in-between state in which some resources are immediately available and some are not. As you may have guessed, this can have a dramatic effect on performance.

In this chapter, we will look at two approaches to configuring WebPageTest such that the results more accurately reflect real-user experiences. First, we will use scripting to address the cache-state gap. Instead of relying on a completely cold cache state on first view and an unrealistically primed cache in the repeat view, we will give instructions to the testing agent to simulate a third state known as the *flow view*. Finally, this chapter will tackle the problem of testing web pages that users are logged into. Many sites personalize content for users, and some pages are entirely blocked off to unauthenticated visitors. In order to get visibility into the performance of these types of pages, we will need to instruct testing agents to log in to a website before running the test.

Flow View

Out of the box, WebPageTest offers two simple yet powerful options to configure a test: first and repeat views. These views are extremely helpful for identifying general performance problems but do not always reflect the state in which a user experiences a page. For example, you may have found through "Popular Pages" on page 59 that most users enter through the home page and navigate to some secondary page.

The resources shared between these two pages (Figure 7-1) would not need to be loaded when the user navigates to the secondary page, assuming that their cache configuration has been set properly. But the remaining resources unique to the secondary page still need to be loaded, and this exact scenario is not always captured by the first or repeat views. So we turn to the scripting interface for finer control.

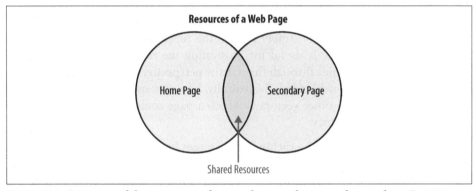

Figure 7-1. Diagram of the resources of two web pages, home and secondary. Between them, there are some shared resources.

logData and navigate

To script the flow view, there are only two basic commands that you need to know:

logData
  Turns on or off the recording of network activity presented by the waterfall diagram.

navigate
  Instructs the test agent to perform an HTTP navigation to a specified URL.

These commands are entered into the scripting input field in the Advanced Settings section, as shown in Figure 7-2.

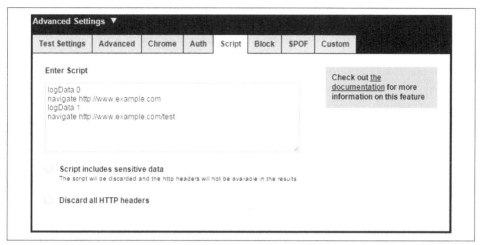

Figure 7-2. WebPageTest is configured to preload the home page of a website before navigating to and capturing the network data for a secondary page

The exact script to perform the flow view is as follows:

```
logData 0
navigate http://www.example.com
logData 1
navigate http://www.example.com/test
```

The first two commands disable network recording and preload the home page. In order to get a clear view of the secondary page's performance, we disable network recording of the home page to exclude it from the waterfall diagram. When the home page is preloaded, all of its cachable resources are warmed up and downloaded for the secondary page to load immediately from cache. The last two commands enable network recording and load the secondary page. Enabling `logData` here ensures that we get the secondary page's network activity in the waterfall diagram. The second `nav igate` command simulates the user clicking on a link from the home page to the */test* page. Resources that have already been loaded on the home page are not reloaded on the secondary page, but rather they are served from cache. In this particular test, we're able to configure WebPageTest to establish the precondition that the home page has been loaded and its resources have been cached. Without scripting, this would not be possible.

By using this simple pattern on pages that are not usually visited directly, test results will more accurately reflect the real-user experience. Remember to look at your RUM report to determine common entry pages and configure your flow views accordingly.

Authentication

Until now, there has been a dangerous blind spot in our performance testing. Our test configurations have all lacked authentication, which is the means by which users are able to log in to a website. Some pages or even the entire site may be completely inaccessible to testing without authentication. Personalization is also an important part of the user experience and it would be important to capture any performance overhead this may incur. For example, simply authenticating a user would typically require a database lookup to verify their credentials. This lookup alone could be a performance bottleneck and would be completely invisible to unauthenticated tests. We need a way to run authenticated tests. Fortunately, WebPageTest provides three ways to do this.

 When testing authenticated pages on WebPageTest, you are strongly advised to use an account specifically for testing purposes. The credentials for this account will be entered into WebPageTest and may be visible on the test results page.

You should also be sure to mark the tests as private, which will prevent the results from appearing in the publicly visible and searchable list of recent test results. Private tests can still be accessed by anyone with the test ID, so the test account credentials may still be exposed inadvertently.

A much more secure defense against leaking account credentials to the public would be to use a private instance of WebPageTest. Refer to Chapter 11 for more information about setting up a private instance.

In this section, we will demonstrate how to use each of the three techniques for enabling test authentication. First, the Auth tab is the most straightforward method. Next, we will utilize the scripting commands to programmatically submit a login form. And finally, we will look at setting an authentication cookie. Even though each approach is designed to produce the same result, we will discuss some caveats that you should consider when selecting a technique.

HTTP Basic Authentication

WebPageTest's advanced configuration section includes a tab specifically for authenticating using a simple HTTP header. The Auth tab allows you to provide a username and password, which is base64-encoded and assigned to an HTTP request header (see Figure 7-3). This technique is called *HTTP Basic Authentication* (HBA).

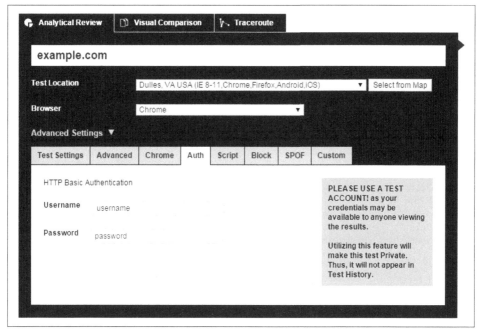

Figure 7-3. In the Advanced Settings section, the Auth tab can be used to input a username and password. This data will be sent to the test page in the form of an Authorization header.

This is the simplest way to configure WebPageTest to log you in as a particular user. Keep in mind, though, that the account credentials are sent in plain text in the HTTP headers. For example, this would be the request header generated by entering a username of `username` and a password of `password` into the Auth tab:

```
Authorization: Basic dXNlcm5hbWU6cGFzc3dvcmQ=
```

The name of the header is `Authorization`, whose value contains text that should be interpreted as account credentials. The `Basic` keyword is a hint to the server how to interpret the encoded value. In this case, the value is a base64-encoded string of a username and password, delimited by a colon. In other words, `dXNlcm5hbWU6cGFzc3dvcmQ=` is `username:password` in base64-encoding. With this data, the server can decode and parse the credentials and authenticate the user.

It's up to the server to support HBA, so this is not always a reliable way to authenticate a test. Still, it is the most straightforward method offered by WebPageTest to log in to a test website.

DOM Manipulation

Another way to authenticate users with WebPageTest is to programmatically interact with the UI of the page to complete a login form. This approach most closely aligns with the way a user would manually log in.

WebPageTest provides several scripting commands that interact with the elements on a page. The two commands that we'll leverage for authentication are `setValue` and `submitForm`:

```
logData 0
navigate http://www.example.com/login
setValue id=u username
setValue id=p password
submitForm id=login-form
logData 1
navigate http://www.example.com/profile/username
```

The way this script works is by first navigating to the login page of our test site without recording any of the activity so far. This should look familiar because this script is an extension of the "Flow View" on page 82, in which one page is loaded before the test page. Next, `setValue` literally sets `username` to be the value of the element with an ID of u. A similar command sets the password on element p. The IDs of these elements are specific to the markup of the login page, so you'll need to inspect the source of the page you're testing. If an ID is not present, you could use any other uniquely identifiable attribute:

```
<input type="text" name="uname" class="form-field">
```

For example, given the preceding HTML, you could use the `name` attribute to target this element directly. There would presumably be many other elements on the page with `type="text"` or `class="form-field"`. The command you would use in this case is:

```
setValue name=uname username
```

As previously mentioned, this script extends the flow view, which means that it is a pseudocached test. One drawback to this approach is that it would not allow you to test a cold load of an authenticated page. This is because the login page's resources will always have been cached first. To address this, we'll look at one final technique that does not require a helper page to log in first.

Setting Cookies

The third and final authentication method is almost a hybrid of the first two methods. Recall that with HBA, the `Authorization` header is included on the initial request. We also tried to manually log in by programmatically mimicking the way a user would complete a form. These methods have their drawbacks: HBA is not supported everywhere, and DOM manipulation requires a login page to be sacrificed to the cache before testing. This method has the simplicity of leveraging HTTP headers and the versatility of using the scripting interface. Here's how it works:

```
setCookie http://www.example.com session=286755fad04869ca523320acce0dc6a4
navigate http://www.example.com/
```

The `setCookie` command enables you to configure a cookie to be included in the request headers. The syntax of the command is `setCookie` *path* *name=value*. The path specifies the domain on which the cookie is valid. After a space delimiter, the path is followed by the name and value of the cookie used to track authenticated users.

This is a hybrid approach because it sets a request header similar to HBA and it uses the scripting interface like the DOM-manipulation approach. However, this is a simple and elegant script unencumbered by the same drawbacks that limit the feasibility of the other techniques. Every website that does authentication will set some kind of cookie to persist the session, so you don't need to worry about lack of support. Conveniently, it is also cold-cache-friendly, so you can get that first-view experience without having to preload a login page.

The beauty of this approach is its extensibility. As written, this is a first-view script with an empty cache, something we were not able to achieve with the DOM-manipulation approach. If necessary, we could incorporate the flow view to get a different caching experience.

CHAPTER 8

SPOF Testing

On November 12, 2014, for 90 excruciating minutes, customers of Google's Double-Click for Publishers (DFP) service experienced an outage. It is estimated that over 50,000 websites were affected, costing millions of dollars in lost advertising revenue. In addition to the direct loss of revenue, there was a secondary effect. Some websites that depended on DFP started experiencing outage-like behavior of their own. Users were unable to access these sites because the pages effectively froze waiting for network activity with the DFP server. This scenario is known as a *single point of failure* (SPOF) of frontend code, in which one weak link can take the whole site down.

> Brian O'Kelley, CEO of AppNexus, operator of a large real-time online ad platform and a DoubleClick rival, estimated the disruption cost publishers $1 million per hour in aggregate.
>
> Wednesday's outages affected more than 55,000 websites, according to Dynatrace, which monitors website and web application performance for companies including eight out of the 10 largest retailers in North America.
>
> —http://on.wsj.com/1EUfDRn

A SPOF is able to happen due to the way browsers handle unresponsive servers. When a server experiences an outage similar to what happened to Google's ad service, websites that depend on it fail to communicate. The browser's normal recourse is to try again. As the browser unsuccessfully attempts to reach the downed server, the original request is left hanging. When this request is made synchronously, all other page activity grinds to a halt.

A user visiting a site that is undergoing a SPOF is likely to have a very bad experience. The page appears blank or incomplete, nothing on the page responds to interactions like scrolling or clicking, and much time is wasted. Users don't care if the site is the victim of a third-party failure; as far as they're concerned, the site is broken. Site owners can immediately expect a loss of business from these users, simply because they're unable to use the site. Worse yet, there are long-term effects that adversely impact these users' sentiment. Sites that go down are seen as less reliable, untrustworthy, and undeserving of a return visit.

There are many possible sources for a SPOF. In addition to the cause in the advertising example, social media widgets are commonly cited examples of SPOF-inducing scripts. A website that includes a button to post to Twitter may suffer if Twitter goes down. Other common third-party resource types include analytics code like Google Analytics and JavaScript frameworks like jQuery. You and your site can be affected if you rely on external resources like these.

You may be thinking at this point that externally hosted third-party resources are terrible because they have the ability to take your website down. Your next thought may be to mitigate the risk of a SPOF by turning these third-party resources into "first-party" resources by hosting them yourself. If the third-party server goes down, you would be unaffected, but if your server goes down, your site would be affected no matter where your resources are hosted. This might seem like a viable alternative, but remember the benefits of third-party resource hosting. Perhaps the most obvious advantage is that you don't have to update the resource as changes are published. For example, some jQuery users prefer to use a centrally located CDN to host the Java-Script file because updates to the library are automatically pushed to the hosted file. Another advantage is that the resource is shared among multiple websites. If the resource is configured to be cached by users, visiting one website will effectively pre-load the resource and make it readily available for the next website. For popular resources, users would rarely need to reload it.

The truth is that third-party resources can be trusted not to bring your site down. Techniques and best practices have been developed to ensure that one server's outage doesn't become everyone else's SPOF. The most straightforward solution is to load third-party resources asynchronously. By definition, this means that the page does not depend on the resource's immediate availability. No matter how long the resource takes to load (even if not at all), the show will go on and the page will continue to function. The feature brought by the resource will be unavailable of course, but developers could plan for that contingency accordingly with fallbacks.

You should be happy to hear that there were many websites that did not go down as a result of that DFP outage. These websites correctly implemented defensive techniques to handle such a failure, and the worst that happened was that the site was unable to display any advertisements. To most users, this sounds like a win. And there certainly were plenty of people rejoicing at the outage for turning a significant portion of the web ad-free. But this is a success story because the problem ended there for these websites. News sites were still able to deliver the news, and ecommerce sites were still able to sell things.

If you weren't eager to start analyzing whether your site is liable to SPOF before, by now you should be. What we've looked at so far with WebPageTest's synthetic testing is good for identifying areas of a page that can be sped up. These tests are somewhat "blue sky" scenarios in which all of your third-party resources' servers are online and properly handling traffic. This presents a blind spot in your analysis if you're looking for potential causes of SPOF. Recall that the other kind of performance measurement, RUM, simply collects live data about how real users are impacted. If a SPOF were to occur, RUM would certainly detect this and show an anomaly in the reporting. But at this point, it's too little too late. The outage is real and your users are suffering for it. What we need is a way to prevent SPOF, not just react to it.

In this chapter, we will look at how to use WebPageTest to diagnose SPOF problems before they happen. To do this, we will induce SPOF-like conditions by preventing responses from ever reaching the client. In this simulation, a request is made and never heard from again, just like what would happen if the server at the other end went down. Using this technique, we hope to expose failure-prone resources that could be costing you valuable business.

We will also discuss request blocking, which is a technique related to inducing SPOF with some clear differences. By preventing requests from ever being dispatched, we are able to measure performance by omission, which is the effect a resource has when removed from the page.

Black-Hole Rerouting

There are only two ways to know how your site reacts to a third-party failure: testing it ahead of time and watching it unfold as it is actually happening. We're going to see how WebPageTest can be used to test third-party failures so that your users aren't the first to know.

The first step of SPOF testing is to identify the third parties that can take your page down. To do this, we use the Domains tab of the results page (Figure 8-1). After running a first-view test of your page, you can access a list of the domains that were used to construct the page. These domains are grouped by the number of requests they served and the total number of bytes sent.

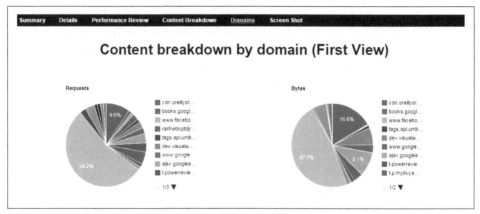

Figure 8-1. The Domains tab of the test results page shows the frequency and size of resources served by each domain for a given page

On this page, we can easily identify the domains that contribute the most to a given test page. Obviously, the domain of the test page itself should be prominently high on the list. What we're looking for are third-party domains out of our control. It would be prudent to test each and every third-party domain for SPOF, but for now let's select the one with the most requests. With this domain, we have a couple of ways to simulate what would happen if it were suddenly inaccessible.

setDns

Recall from "Reading a Waterfall" on page 10 that DNS lookup is just the resolution of a recognizable hostname like *example.com* to its IP address. This process is identical to looking up a phone number in a phone book. With DNS resolution, there are many phone books: some are little black books while others are exhaustive tomes. Computers have their own little black book in which to jot down a few important names and numbers. If the browser needs to resolve a name not in this book, it asks an authoritative DNS server. WebPageTest provides a way for you to jot any name and number into its little black book. You don't even need to use the correct number for the given name. This is exactly what we'll do to simulate our first SPOF.

To test what happens when a given domain goes offline, start by opening up the familiar Script tab. This time we're going to use a new command, setDns:

```
setDns _domain_ _IP address_
navigate _test URL_
```

The setDns command designates an IP address to be the point of contact for all requests to a given domain. When navigating to a test page, any requests at the given domain will route to the given address. Now we need an IP address that points to a server that pretends to be failing. WebPageTest has you covered with the appropri-

---

ately named *blackhole.webpagetest.org* host. By assigning this host's IP address to a domain, we're able to simulate its failure:

blackhole.webpagetest.org
    72.66.115.13

It's worth noting that when you run a SPOF test, nothing may actually go wrong. This is a good thing! This means that your page is adequately prepared to handle the sudden failure of a third-party resource. When this isn't the case, the test results speak for themselves (Figure 8-2).

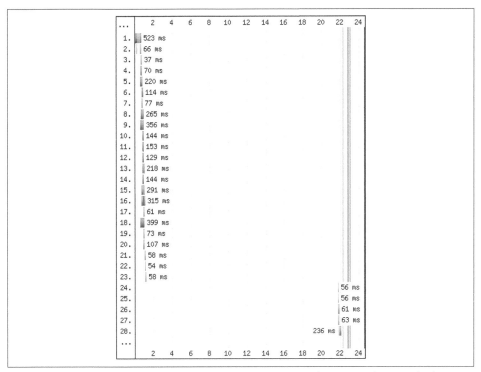

Figure 8-2. The failure of a resource resulted in a 20-second timeout, during which no other requests were able to be made and page loading halted

The waterfall diagram clearly shows a gap 20 seconds long between requests. This is the amount of time that the browser spent attempting to communicate with the third party. Instead of communicating with the third party, though, the browser was sending requests to the black hole without receiving any responses. During this time, the browser is not able to start any other requests. If this happens early enough, the user would be left with an incomplete, possibly unresponsive page.

SPOF Tab

If you're thinking that scripting is a cumbersome way to run a SPOF test, you should be relieved to know that WebPageTest makes it even easier. With the SPOF advanced settings tab (Figure 8-3), all you need to do is enter the domain that you want to send to the black hole.

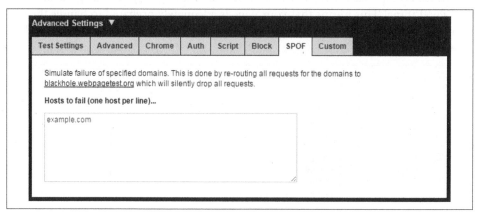

Figure 8-3. The SPOF tab allows you to test the failure of a domain without having to write a setDns script

When you run a test from the SPOF tab, you're actually running two tests: one with and without the DNS override. By running a normal test along with the SPOF test, you have a control to differentiate the effects of the simulation. Instead of taking you to the individual test results when the test is complete, the SPOF test results are displayed in the comparison view, as shown in Figure 8-4. This makes it extremely easy to identify the user-perceived effects of a SPOF. WebPageTest also generates a video comparison of the normal page load and the effects of SPOF, as shown in Figure 8-5.

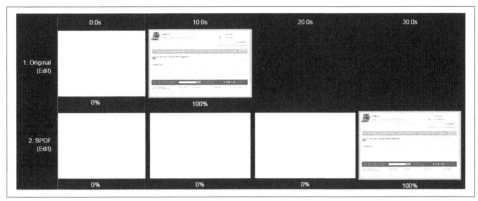

Figure 8-4. The SPOF tab generates a comparison of tests with and without domain failures. The filmstrip view clearly shows the page-load impact of SPOF in which the SPOF page takes more than 20 seconds longer to load.

When we look at the filmstrip comparison of the two tests, the 20-second difference is immediately apparent. Other metrics like visual progress and speed index also illustrate the dramatic consequences of a request timing out. See Figure 8-6 for a visual progress chart.

Figure 8-5. WebPageTest also generates a video comparison of each test so that you can watch a page load normally and observe the effects of SPOF side-by-side

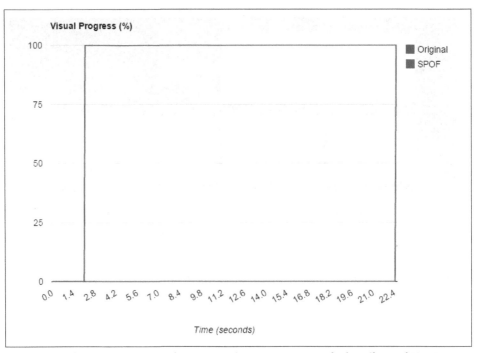

Figure 8-6. The visual progress chart is another way to quantify the effects of SPOF on a page. This chart compares the amount of time it takes for a page to display its content. Under SPOF conditions, the progress is 0% for more than 20 seconds until the failed request times out and the page load is able to complete.

Using the SPOF tab is an incredibly convenient way to demonstrate the dangers of the irresponsible use of third-party resources. Developers should never assume that third parties are 100% reliable, because anything can happen, even to the biggest Internet giants.

Blocking Requests

SPOF is such a dramatic scenario. The weakest link in a chain of requests could spell destruction for the usability of an entire page. Failure in this case is a third-party meltdown improperly handled on the client side. Sometimes failure could just be a resource that is too slow. *Service-level agreements* (SLAs) are used by some third parties to reassure dependents that they will serve resources at some high rate of reliability or even no slower than some guaranteed speed. Failure could also be an SLA that wasn't met. It doesn't take a total meltdown for users to become annoyed at the slowness of page load; resources that load more slowly than expected can and should be considered failures.

How can we measure the impact of a particular resource? As we know, the time it takes to load a resource is only part of the story. For JavaScript resources, there is also time to parse and execute the code. The simplest way to measure a resource would be to run tests of a page with and without it. The difference in speed is the residual effect of that resource.

A practical example of this is advertisements. Ads are generally regarded as a necessary evil, so we may be too quick to accept the performance hit they incur. One way to measure their impact would be to serve pages without ads to some segment of users and compare performance against a control group. Unfortunately, ads are what keep the lights on, and it may be extremely difficult to convince the powers that be to voluntarily give up ad revenue to an entire segment of users. Instead of a RUM A/B test, we can use synthetic testing to simulate a page with and without ads.

WebPageTest exposes the functionality to block requests based on pattern matching. For example, you could instruct the test agent to prevent resource names containing the "ads" substring from being requested. This functionality is exposed in the script tab through the block command.

```
block _substring_
navigate _test URL_
```

Any request for a URL containing the substring will be blocked from ever reaching the network (Figure 8-7). How is this any different from sending the request into the black hole? Most important, browsers will not timeout on a request that was never made, so the page will not experience that long pause between requests. This test simply measures the omission of a resource without presuming anything about its reliability or load time.

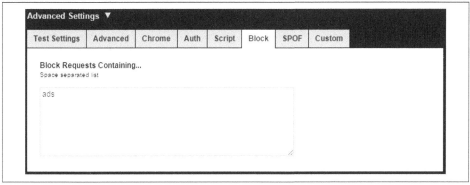

Figure 8-7. The block tab takes a space-delimited list of substrings to be matched against blocked requests. If the request URL contains any of these substrings, it will be prevented from materializing.

If scripting is not your thing, take comfort in the fact that WebPageTest has a tab for blocking requests, too. This one couldn't be simpler to use; just enter one or more substrings to match against requests that should be blocked.

As with any synthetic test, several runs are essential to ensuring that the results are accurate and representative. Nine test runs with and without blocking should be enough to get a suitable median run that could be used for comparison.

Advanced Use Cases

So far we have looked at how to use WebPageTest to configure and analyze synthetic web performance tests. We started by learning what the test results mean and how to read a waterfall. In Part II, we learned how to fine-tune the test configuration to more accurately reflect real-use cases and how to simulate anomalies like third-party outages. Until now, everything has gone through the public WebPageTest UI.

Part III is all about advanced use cases of WebPageTest. The users who will benefit the most from this unit are enterprise-level developers who have very high demand for test automation and monitoring, especially for prerelease web applications. In the following chapters, we will look at the application programming interface (API) of WebPageTest and use it to run tests and get test results. We will also cover the process of getting a local version of WebPageTest to run privately on our own machine. Using these concepts, you will be able to leverage the versatility of WebPageTest for even the most demanding requirements for synthetic testing.

CHAPTER 9

WebPageTest API

The WebPageTest API is RESTful, meaning that commands with parameters are submitted by either sending a POST or GET request to WebPageTest server PHP endpoints. The API is not fully normalized; output formats vary from endpoint to endpoint. The vast majority output JSON/JSONP and XML, but some output CSV, TSV, HTML, and plain text. The WebPageTest UI uses its API, so every command and option found on the user interface has a correspondent in the API.

In this chapter you will learn how to programatically run tests and fetch results from WebPageTest in both public and private instances. This will allow integration with an existing web development pipeline, as well as the automation of the whole process of running a test and reading its results once the test is complete.

Getting Started

Before getting ready to start using the WebPageTest API, you will need direct access to either the public instance of the WebPageTest server at *www.webpagetest.org* or a private instance of WebPageTest, covered in Chapter 11.

Requesting a Key

An API key is required for using the public instance at *www.webpagetest.org*. It's generally not necessary for private instances of WebPageTest unless required by its administrator. The API key is only used by the run-test endpoint /runtest.php.

Public instance

For the public instance, a trial key can be obtained by filling out a form at *http:// www.webpagetest.org/getkey.php*.

Agreeing with the terms of service is required as the service is offered on a best-effort basis and there are no guarantees on anything.

After you submit the form, an email with information on how to retrieve an API key is sent to you.

API key limitations

The use of an API key on the public instance of the WebPageTest server is subject to the following limitations:

- The API key is provisioned for up to 200 page loads per day. Each run (of first and repeat views) counts as a page load (10 runs of both first and repeat views would count as 20 page loads). That should be sufficient for most low-volume use cases and for building a proof-of-concept for larger testing.

- API keys are limited to testing from a subset of locations: Amazon Elastic Compute Cloud (EC2) regions and the Dulles Chrome, Firefox, IE, and Mobile agents. The EC2 locations will offer consistent performance from location to location and can be scaled as necessary to meet demand.

- The results for tests run with an API key are only available for 30 days from when the test was run.

If more testing, other locations, or longer availability is needed, a private instance should be considered. There are prepackaged Amazon Machine Images (AMIs) available on EC2 for running a full WebPageTest instance.

Private instance

On private instances where an API key is required, the server administrator should be able to provide one defined in the *settings/keys.ini* file, which optionally provides the following defaults and limitations:

Default location
WebPageTest allows a default location and browser to be assigned to a given API key via the `default location` property. Tests submitted without a specific location will use the one defined for a given API key rather than a global one defined in *settings/locations.ini*.

Quota
Usage quota, i.e., number of page loads allowed per day, can be restricted per API key via the `limit` property, giving more granular control and preventing test abuse.

Priority

Test priority can be enforced per API key via the `priority` property, which over-rides any priority informed when scheduling a test with any `priority` parameter.

Queue limit

By default, there is no limit for queueing tests for a given API key unless the `queue_limit` property is defined.

Running Tests

In order to run a test, you must provide a minimum set of configurations so that the test can be queued to run when an agent that matches that configuration is available. The following examples assume that the reader has an API key to run tests on a public instance of WebPageTest.

Simple Example Test

Here we will run a web performance test of *http://www.example.com* on a WebPageTest public instance using an API key with the default configuration and returning results in JSON.

The first step is to make a request to the WebPageTest server to queue the web performance test of *http://www.example.com*, providing an API key and setting the output format as JSON:

```
http://www.webpagetest.org/runtest.php?url=http%3A%2F%2Fwww.example.com
    &k=API_KEY_GOES_HERE&f=json
```

Breaking down the preceding URL:

Protocol
    `http`

Server host
    `www.webpagetest.org` (public instance)

API endpoint
    `/runtest.php`

Parameters (key=value)

   Web page to be tested
       `url=http%3A%2F%2Fwww.example.com` (value must be UTF-8 encoded)

   API key
       `k=API_KEY_GOES_HERE`

Output format
```
f=json
```

If the test is queued successfully, the WebPageTest server will return the following JSON response:

```
{
  "statusCode": 200,
  "statusText": "Ok",
  "data": {
    "testId": "150109_DE_ZW7",
    "ownerKey": "0123456789abcdef0123456789abcdef01234567",
    "jsonUrl": "http://www.webpagetest.org/jsonResult.php?test=150109_DE_ZW7",
    "xmlUrl": "http://www.webpagetest.org/xmlResult/150109_DE_ZW7/",
    "userUrl": "http://www.webpagetest.org/result/150109_DE_ZW7/",
    "summaryCSV": "http://www.webpagetest.org/result/150109_DE_ZW7/page_data.csv",
    "detailCSV": "http://www.webpagetest.org/result/150109_DE_ZW7/requests.csv"
  }
}
```

Where:

`statusCode`
    Code indicating that test was accepted and queued successfully

`statusText`
    A human-readable response confirming test was accepted and queued

`data`
    The response object with some information about the test recently queued:

    `testId`
        The unique identifier for the queued test (most useful data)

    `ownerKey`
        A SHA-1 hash unique identifier for the request

    `jsonUrl`
        The API endpoint to retrieve the test results in JSON format

    `xmlUrl`
        The API endpoint to retrieve the test results in XML format

    `userUrl`
        The URL for the WebPageTest user interface (HTML) with test results

    `summaryCSV`
        The URL for the test summary in CSV format

detailCSV
>The URL for the details of all requests in the tested page in CSV format

The `testId` is the key used to retrieve any data for the just-queued test. URLs in `jsonUrl`, `xmlUrl`, or `userUrl` will return test results (covered in "Reading the Results" on page 107) if the test is complete, the status of the test informing which position in queue if not started yet, or how long since the test has been started.

Status codes

10x
>Test not ready

>100
>>Test started

>101
>>Test in queue

>102
>>Server unreacheable

200
>Test complete

40x
>Error

>400
>>Test not found

>401
>>Test request not found (valid `testId` but not found in work queues)

>402
>>Test canceled

If you are running from a private instance where an API key might not be required to run tests, the API request is even simpler:

```
http://private-instance/runtest.php?url=http%3A%2F%2Fwww.example.com&f=json
```

Advanced Example Test

`/runtest.php` is the API endpoint with the largest number of parameters. This is due to how the API workflow works; i.e., it all starts from configuring a test to be run by a WebPageTest agent. Once the test is done, the other API endpoints are as simple as informing the test ID to retrieve data. The following example will request the public instance of WebPageTest to run a test for *http://www.example.com* with the following configuration:

- Run from San Francisco location
- Use latest Chrome
- Use DSL connectivity profile
- Run three times
- First view only (for each run)
- Capture video
- Set "Using WebPageTest" as test label
- Capture DevTools Timeline information

```
http://www.webpagetest.org/runtest.php?url=http%3A%2F%2Fwww.example.com
    &k=API_KEY_GOES_HERE&location=SanFrancisco%3AChrome.DSL
      &connectivity=DSL&runs=3&fvonly=1&video=1&label=Using%20WebPagetest
        &timeline=1&f=json
```

Breaking down the preceding URL:

Protocol
    http

Server host
    www.webpagetest.org (public instance)

API endpoint
    /runtest.php

Parameters (key=value)

   Web page to be tested
       url=http%3A%2F%2Fwww.example.com (value must be UTF-8 encoded)

   API key
       k=*API_KEY_GOES_HERE*

   Location
       location=SanFrancisco%3AChrome.DSL (in the format: Location-Name:BrowserName.ConnectivityProfile, value must be UTF-8 encoded)

   Connectivity profile
       connectivity=DSL

   Number of runs
       runs=3

First view only
```
fvonly=1
```

Capture video
```
video=1
```

Test label
```
label=Using%20WebPageTest
```
(value must be UTF-8 encoded)

Capture DevTools timeline
```
timeline=1
```

Output format
```
f=json
```

Reading the Results

Reading the results is as simple as informing the testId to /jsonResult.php
or /xmlResult.php API endpoints with the test=*testId* parameter.

```
http://www.webpagetest.org/jsonResult.php?test=150109_DE_ZW7
```

If the test is not yet complete, the WebPageTest server may return:

```
{
  "data": {
    "statusCode": 100,
    "statusText": "Test Started 4 seconds ago",
    "id": "150109_DE_ZW7",
    "testInfo": {
      "url": "http://www.example.com",
      // More information about the test. See Appendix A.
    },
    "testId": "150109_DE_ZW7",
    "runs": 1,
    "fvonly": 0,
    "remote": false,
    "testsExpected": 1,
    "location": "Dulles:Chrome",
    "startTime": "01/09/15 17:51:16",
    "elapsed": 4,
    "fvRunsCompleted": 0,
    "rvRunsCompleted": 0,
    "testsCompleted": 0
  },
  "statusCode": 100,
  "statusText": "Test Started 4 seconds ago"
}
```

The statusCode of 100 indicates that the test has started as statusText, and elapsed
shows 4 seconds. testInfo shows details about the test configuration. If the test has

multiple runs, `fvRunsCompleted` (first view) and `rvRunsCompleted` (repeat view) should increment up to `testsExpected` until the test is complete and `statusCode` is 200.

When the test is complete, WebPageTest returns exhaustive test results containing test information as well as performance metrics for the tested page. For conciseness, some result properties were omitted from the following JSON response, and similar properties were replaced by comments. See Appendix A for more information.

```
{
  "data": {
    "id": "150109_DE_ZW7",
    "url": "http://www.example.com",
    "summary": "http://www.webpagetest.org/results.php?test=150109_DE_ZW7",
    "location": "Dulles:Chrome",
    "runs": {
      "1": {
        "firstView": {
          "URL": "http://www.example.com",
          "loadTime": 194,
          // See Appendix A for exhaustive results info.
        }
      },
      "fvonly": false,
      "successfulFVRuns": 1,
      "successfulRVRuns": 1,
      "average": {
        "firstView": {
          // similar to data.runs.1.firstView above but without pages,
          // thumbnails, images, rawData, videoFrames, domains and breakdown
        },
        "repeatView": {
          // similar to data.runs.average.firstView above
        }
      },
      "standardDeviation": {
        // similar to data.runs.average above
      },
      "median": {
        // similar to data.runs.1 above
      }
    },
    "statusCode": 200,
    "statusText": "Test Complete"
  }
}
```

Test result properties might change in new releases of WebPageTest. Metrics might be added, removed, renamed, or moved. Check WebPageTest releases (*https://github.com/WPO-Foundation/webpagetest/releases*) for the latest.

Reading results is usually done in an automatic fashion once the test is succesfully queued by /runtest.php. There are two ways to automate the process of reading results: polling and pingback.

Polling Test Results

Polling is when a client sends a request to the server over and over to check whether it has the expected data. With this method, the WebPageTest server /jsonResult.php, /xmlResult.php or /testStatus.php API endpoints will be hit several times until statusCode is 200. The /testStatus.php endpoint will not return test results when the test is complete; therefore, it is easier and safer to hit the /jsonResult.php or /xmlResult.php endpoints to get test results when status Code is 200. This will save a round-trip to the WebPageTest server. More information about the /testStatus.php endpoint can be found in Appendix A.

The following example implements a simple polling mechanism in JavaScript. It requests a WebPageTest public instance to test *http://www.example.com* using the default test configuration and then polls test results at every five seconds:

```
var
  URL_TO_TEST = 'http://www.example.com',
  WPT_API_KEY = 'API_KEY_GOES_HERE',
  WPT_RUNTEST_URL = 'http://www.webpagetest.org/runtest.php?url=%s&k=%s&f=json',
  WPT_RESULTS_URL = 'http://www.webpagetest.org/jsonResult.php?test=%s';

function wpt(url, callback) {
  window._callback = callback;
  var script = document.createElement('script');
  script.src = url + '&callback=_callback';
  document.head.appendChild(script);
  document.head.removeChild(script);
}

function results(res) {
  if (res.statusCode == 200) {
  console.log('First Paint:', res.data.median.firstView.firstPaint);
  } else if (res.statusCode < 200) {
    var testId = res.data.id;
    console.log('Test', testId, 'not ready yet. Trying again in 5s');
    setTimeout(wpt, 5000, WPT_RESULTS_URL.replace('%s', testId), results);
  }
}

function runTest(res) {
  var testId = res.data.testId;
  console.log('Test', testId, 'requested. Start polling in 5s');
  setTimeout(wpt, 5000, WPT_RESULTS_URL.replace('%s', testId), results);
}
```

```
var url = encodeURIComponent(URL_TO_TEST);
wpt(WPT_RUNTEST_URL.replace('%s', url).replace('%s', WPT_API_KEY), runTest);
```

 The previous code example is an oversimplification for browser console testing purposes only. It is not intended to be production-ready in any way.

Pingback Test Results

WebPageTest can also indicate when a test is complete. This is called *pingback* and avoids unnecessary round-trips to the server (unlike polling). By providing a URL to the `pingback` parameter of the `/runTest.php` endpoint, WebPageTest will hit that URL with `?test=test_id` when the test is complete.

In order for the WebPageTest server (both public and private instances) to be able to pingback when the test is complete, the `pingback` URL must be accessible from the WebPageTest server. This means that if the `pingback` URL is behind a proxy, firewall, or private network to which WebPageTest has no direct access, the `pingback` URL will not be hit when the test is complete.

The following example implements a simple pingback mechanism in JavaScript. It requests a WebPageTest public instance to test *http://www.example.com* using the default test configuration with pingback set to a given RequestBin URL. In order to test the following code on a browser console, a free RequestBin URL must be created at *http://requestb.in*.

```
var
    URL_TO_TEST = 'http://www.example.com',
    WPT_API_KEY = 'API_KEY_GOES_HERE',
    REQUEST_BIN_URL = 'REQUEST_BIN_URL_GOES_HERE', // Get one at http://requestb.in
    WPT_RUNTEST_URL = 'http://www.webpagetest.org/runtest.php?url=%s&k=%s&f=json',

function wpt(url) {
    var script = document.createElement('script');
    url += '&callback=console.log';
    script.src = url + '&pingback=' + encodeURIComponent(REQUEST_BIN_URL);
    document.head.appendChild(script);
    document.head.removeChild(script);
    var requestBinUrl = REQUEST_BIN_URL + '?inspect';
    console.log('Test requested. Check', requestBinUrl, 'later');
    window.open(requestBinUrl, '_blank');
}

var url = encodeURIComponent(URL_TO_TEST);
wpt(WPT_RUNTEST_URL.replace('%s', url).replace('%s', WPT_API_KEY));
```

The previous code example is an oversimplification for browser console testing purposes only. It is not intended to be production-ready in any way.

Although pingback eliminates extra round-trips to the WebPageTest server, polling is generally more reliable, because WebPageTest may fail to inform the pingback URL when the test is complete. If the pingback URL takes too long to be hit, it is unknown if the test is really taking that long or if pingback failed. Polling always knows the current test status, which allows a reliable timeout mechanism to be set. Another option is to use both methods: pingback, and then after a certain timeout, start polling.

Reading Beyond Results

/runTest.php and /jsonResult.php or /xmlResult.php are the essential WebPageTest API endpoints. They allow the entire testing-and-reading-results workflow for the vast majority of automation with WebPageTest. There are other API endpoints for reading specific details of a test, such as /export.php to get the complete HAR (HTTP Archive), /getTimeline.php to get DevTools timeline data from tests performed by the Chrome browser, and /getgzip.php to retrieve several other types of test data. For a WebPageTest private instance, /getLocations.php and /getTesters.php can be used to automate the process of maintenance. Both retrive important information about the status of test locations and their agents.

See the WebPageTest RESTful APIs documentation (*https:// sites.google.com/a/webpagetest.org/docs/advanced-features/ webpagetest-restful-apis*) for information on running tests and reading results. For the complete list of WebPageTest API endpoints, including undocumented ones, check Appendix A.

So far, we manually hit WebPageTest endpoints to run tests and read results. These are the WebPageTest API core endpoints. You are now able to adapt and integrate the code examples from this chapter into your own web development pipeline as needed. Chapter 10, however, will provide easier and seamless ways to automate this process.

Continuous Integration

In software engineering, *continuous integration* (CI) can be defined as the practice of merging all developer working copies with a shared repository several times a day. It performs automated unit tests in build servers to improve software quality through frequent small efforts.

WebPageTest can be integrated into a CI pipeline to test web pages in the build or staging server. It can be used to indicate when the performance of web pages has regressed. Such integration can be done by customizing the running and reading of tests, as described in Chapter 9.

A common workflow would be to run WebPageTest after the CI pipeline successfully builds and all unit tests pass. Using either polling or pingback to retrieve WebPageTest results, some metrics from the full results set should be compared against expected metrics. For example, `data.median.firstView.firstPaint` must be less than 800 ms, or `data.median.firstView.domElements` must be between 800 and 1,000.

In this chapter, you will first learn how to consume WebPageTest API endpoints via the command line or as a Node.js application. You will also learn how to easily automate the whole process of running a test and reading its results in order to integrate with some popular CI tools.

Node.js Wrapper

`webpagetest` is a Node.js package available on NPM (package manager for Node.js). It provides a wrapper around the WebPageTest RESTful API with the following features:

- Normalizes API endpoints and parameter names with JSON response

- Command-line tool with both short and long options
- Methods with asynchronous callback function for Node.js applications
- Polling and pingback helpers to run tests and read results synchronously
- Command-line batch jobs
- WebPageTest RESTful API proxy
- WebPageTest scripting helper
- CI test specs

The `webpagetest` Node.js wrapper is an open souce project under MIT license and lives on GitHub at *https://github.com/marcelduran/webpagetest-api*.

Installing the WebPageTest Node.js Wrapper

Assuming Node.js is already installed, type the following at the command prompt:

```
npm install webpagetest -g
```

The `-g` is required to make the command line available.

Once the WebPageTest Node.js Wrapper is installed, you have the command line available in your terminal and can get more information by typing:

```
webpagetest --help
```

Choosing Your WebPageTest Server

The default WebPageTest API Wrapper server is the public instance (*www.webpagetest.org*), but you can override it in the command line by doing one of two things:

- Setting the `-s, -server` *server* option—for example, `webpagetest -s wpt-private-server.com`
- Setting the `WEBPAGETEST_SERVER` environment variable—for example, `export WEBPAGETEST_SERVER=wpt-private-server.com`

As a Node.js module, the default WebPageTest server is also the public instance and can be overridden by specifying the first parameter of the constructor:

```
var WebPagetest = require('webpagetest');

var publicWPT = new WebPagetest();

var privateWPT = new WebPagetest('wpt-private-server.com');
```

Even when a WebPageTest server is specified, you can still override it with any method by supplying the server option:

```
var wpt = new WebPagetest('wpt-private-server.com');

wpt.getLocations({server: 'another-wpt-server.com'}, function(err, data) {
  console.log(err || data);
});
```

Specifying the API Key

To specify the API key in the command line in order to run a test, set the `-k`, `-key` *api_key* as follows:

```
webpagetest -k API_KEY_GOES_HERE test http://www.example.com
```

As a Node.js module, it can be set either as the second parameter in the constructor function or as an option in the `runTest` function:

```
var wpt = new WebPagetest('wpt-private-server.com', 'API_KEY_GOES_HERE');

// run test on wpt-private-server.com with a given API key
wpt.runTest('http://www.example.com', function(err, data) {
  console.log(err || data);
});

// run test on wpt-private-server.com with another given API key
wpt.runTest('http://www.example.com', {key: 'ANOTHER_API_KEY'}, function(
    err, data) {
  console.log(err || data);
});
```

Running the Tests and Reading the Results

Following the examples from Chapter 9, testing with the WebPageTest API Wrapper is cleaner and easier.

Running tests from the command line

To test the web performance of *http://www.example.com* on a WebPageTest public instance using an API key with default configuration:

```
webpagetest test http://www.example.com -k API_KEY_GOES_HERE
```

Or with long parameter names:

```
webpagetest test http://www.example.com --key API_KEY_GOES_HERE
```

Here's the same test but with the following configuration:

- Run from San Francisco location
- Use latest Chrome
- Use DSL connectivity profile

- Run three times
- First view only (for each run)
- Capture video
- Set "Using WebPageTest" as test label
- Capture DevTools Timeline information

```
webpagetest test http://www.example.com -k API_KEY_GOES_HERE -l \
SanFrancisco:Chrome -y DSL -r 3 -f -v -L "Using WebPageTest" -M
```

Or with long parameter names:

```
webpagetest test http://www.example.com --key API_KEY_GOES_HERE --location \
SanFrancisco:Chrome --connectivity DSL --runs 3 --first --video --label \
"Using WebPageTest" --timeline
```

Batch jobs can be run in parallel while the response follows the same order as in a given input file. Assuming *jobs.txt* has the following content:

```
test http://www.example.com -k API_KEY_GOES_HERE
webpagetest test http://www.example.com -k API_KEY_GOES_HERE -l \
SanFrancisco:Chrome -y DSL -r 3 -f -v -L "Using WebPageTest" -M
```

Then from the command line, type:

```
webpagetest batch jobs.txt
```

The test command also supports a WebPageTest script file as input instead of a URL. Assuming *sample.wptscript* has the following content:

```
logData 0
navigate http://www.example.com/login
logData 1
setValue name=username johndoe
setValue name=password 12345
submitForm action=http://www.example.com/main
waitForComplete
```

Then from command line, type:

```
webpagetest test sample.wptscript
```

Reading results from the command line

To read results, assuming any of the above test commands returned 150109_DE_ZW7 as testId, type:

```
webpagetest results 150109_DE_ZW7
```

Running tests and reading results from the command line

Since running a test and then reading its results is the most common WebPageTest workflow, the Node.js wrapper provides polling and pingback mechanisms. Here is an example that requests that a WebPageTest public instance test the web performance of *http://www.example.com* using the default test configuration, and then start polling every five seconds (default interval that can be overriden if a number in seconds is provided for the - -poll parameter):

```
webpagetest test http://www.example.com -k API_KEY_GOES_HERE --poll
```

Here's the same example pinging back to a private instance of WebPageTest, because a public instance wouldn't be able to pingback localhost:

```
webpagetest test http://www.example.com -s wpt-private-server.com --wait
```

For both of these tests, - -timeout could be provided (in seconds) to either stop polling or abandon waiting for pingback.

Running tests and reading results from a Node.js module

All methods are asynchronous; i.e., they require a callback function that is executed when the WebPageTest API response is received with either data or an error. Unlike with the command line, method names on the Node.js module are verbose (e.g., get TestResults versus results) for code readability.

The following example tests the web performance of *http://www.example.com* on a WebPageTest public instance using an API key with the default configuration, and then polls results every five seconds, getting the first-paint time for first view:

```
var WebPagetest = require('webpagetest');

var wpt = new WebPagetest('www.webpagetest.org', 'API_KEY_GOES_HERE');

wpt.runTest('http://www.example.com', function(err, res) {
  if (err || res.statusCode >= 400) {
    return console.log(err || res.statusText);
  }
  function results(err, res) {
    if (res.statusCode < 200) {
      console.log('Test', res.data.id, 'not ready yet. Trying again in 5s');
      setTimeout(wpt.getTestResults.bind(wpt, res.data.id, results), 5000);
    } else if (res.statusCode == 200) {
      console.log('First Paint:', res.data.median.firstView.firstPaint);
    }
  }
  console.log('Test', res.data.testId, 'requested. Start polling in 5s');
  setTimeout(wpt.getTestResults.bind(wpt, res.data.testId, results), 5000);
});
```

This could be simplified using the pollResults option:

```
var WebPagetest = require('webpagetest');

var wpt = new WebPagetest('www.webpagetest.org', 'API_KEY_GOES_HERE');
```

```
wpt.runTest('http://www.example.com', {pollResults: 5}, function(err, res) {
  console.log(err || 'First Paint: ' + res.data.median.firstView.firstPaint);
});
```

Similarly, pingback coud also be used in the previous example:

```
var WebPagetest = require('webpagetest'),
    os = require('os'),
    url = require('url'),
    http = require('http');

var wpt = new WebPagetest('wpt-private-server.com');

// Local server to listen for test complete.
var localServer = http.createServer(function(req, res) {
  var uri = url.parse(req.url, true);

  res.end();

  // Get test results.
  if (uri.pathname === '/testdone' && uri.query.id) {
    localServer.close(function() {
      wpt.getTestResults(uri.query.id, function(err, res) {
        console.log(err || 'First Paint: ' + res.data.median.firstView.firstPaint);
      });
    });
  }
});

// Test http://www.example.com.
wpt.runTest('http://www.example.com', {
  pingback: url.format({
    protocol: 'http',
    hostname: os.hostname(),
    port: 8080,
    pathname: '/testdone'
  })
}, function(err, data) {
  // Listen for test complete (pingback).
  localServer.listen(8080);
});
```

Or to make it even simpler, use the `waitResults` option:

```
var WebPagetest = require('webpagetest');

var wpt = new WebPagetest('wpt-private-server.com');

wpt.runTest('http://www.example.com', {waitResults: 'auto'}, function(err, res) {
  console.log(err || 'First Paint: ' + res.data.median.firstView.firstPaint);
});
```

By setting `auto` to `waitResults`, the WebPageTest Node.js Wrapper uses `system host name` as the hostname and `8000` as the port, which is incremented by 1 in case the port is in use.

 In the previous examples, the pingback URL must be reachable from the private WebPageTest server, aliased as *wpt-private-server.com*.

The `timeout` option is also available for both `pollResults` and `waitResults` functions.

To avoid the error-prone hassle of tabs versus spaces, the WebPageTest API Wrapper provides a script builder function named `scriptToString`:

```
var script = wpt.scriptToString([
  {logData: 0},
  {navigate: 'http://www.example.com/login'},
  {logData: 1},
  {setValue: ['name=username', 'johndoe']},
  {setValue: ['name=password', '12345']},
  {submitForm: 'action=http://www.example.com/main'},
  'waitForComplete'
]);
wpt.runTest(script, function (err, data) {
  console.log(err || data);
});
```

RESTful Proxy

The WebPageTest API Wrapper comes with a handy RESTful proxy (listener) that exposes WebPageTest API methods consistently. It means that all the benefits of methods, options, and JSON output from the WebPageTest API Wrapper can be easily reachable through RESTful endpoints.

API proxy endpoints follow the format:

/command[*/main_parameter*>][?parameter1=value1&parameter2=value2&...]

where:

- command: One of the available commands (`test`, `results`, etc.) from the command line
- main_parameter: Usually a `test_id`, `url`, or `wpt_script`

- parameter=value: List of extra optional parameters—for example, key, first, etc.

Running a proxy from the command line

Assuming a WebPageTest private instance is located at *wpt-private-server.com* and a local machine named `local-machine` has bidirectional direct access:

```
webpagetest listen --server wpt-private-server.com
```

This will turn the local machine into a WebPageTest API Wrapper RESTful proxy for *wpt-private-server.com*. From any other machine in the same network, WebPageTest can be accessed via RESTful proxy, such as:

http://local-machine/help
  Displays the WebPageTest API Wrapper help (use *http://local-machine/help/<command>* to get help for a given command).

http://local-machine/locations
  Fetches WebPageTest locations for *wpt-private-server.com*.

http://local-machine/test/http%3A%2F%2Fwww.example.com.com?first=true
  Runs a test for *http://www.example.com* using default test configuration on *wpt-private-server.com*.

http://local-machine/results/150109_DE_ZW7
  Fetches test results for an existing test with ID 150109_DE_ZW7 on *wpt-private-server.com*.

If `--server` or `-s` is not provided, the WebPageTest API Wrapper first checks the `WEBPAGETEST_SERVER` environment variable and falls back to the public instance, *www.webpagetest.org*.

Running a proxy from a Node.js module

The method for running a proxy from a Node.js module is called `listen` and has one optional port parameter (default 7791).

```
var WebPageTest = require('webpagetest');
var wpt = new WebPageTest();
wpt.listen(3000);
```

Asserting Metrics from Test Results

The WebPageTest API Wrapper introduces the concept of test specs. It allows any test result coming from the `results` command directly or from synchronous tests with --

poll or --wait options to be asserted by comparing the actual result with expected results defined by a spec JSON string or file.

JSON Test Specs

The *assertion test specs* file follows the structure of the JSON output of the WebPageTest results command. Starting from data as the root node, it traverses the entire result tree looking for matching leaves from the *test specs definition* file.

As an example, assume that a JSON file named *testspecs.json* has the following test specs definition:

```
{
  "median": {
    "firstView": {
      "requests": 20,
      "render": 400,
      "loadTime": 3000,
      "score_gzip": {
        "min": 90
      }
    }
  }
}
```

If we run the following command to test the first view of *http://staging.example.com* using polling and specifying the previous test specs:

```
webpagetest test http://staging.example.com --first --poll
  --specs testspecs.json
```

The test returns the following test results:

```
{
  "data": {
  ...
    "median": {
      "firstView": {
        ...
        "requests": 15,
        "render": 500,
        "loadTime": 2500,
        "score_gzip": 70
        ...
      }
    },
    ...
  }
}
```

It is then compared to *testspecs.json* and the output is:

```
WebPageTest
    ✓ median.firstView.requests: 15 should be less than 20
    1) median.firstView.render: 500 should be less than 400
    ✓ median.firstView.loadTime: 2500 should be less than 3000
    2) median.firstView.score_gzip: 70 should be greater than 90


  2 passing (3 ms)
  2 failing
```

The exit status is:

```
echo $?
2
```

Defining Assertion Comparison

By default, all comparison operations are < (less than), except when an object is informed with min and/or max values. In this case, the operations used for comparison are > (greater than) and < (less than) when both min and max are informed that a range comparison is used.

Examples of overriding assertion comparison

Less-than comparison:

```
{ "median": { "firstView": {
  "render": 400
}}}
```

or

```
{ "median": { "firstView": {
  "render": { "max": 400 }
}}}
```

Greater-than comparison:

```
{ "median": { "firstView": {
  "score_gzip": { "min": 75 }
}}}
```

Range comparison:

```
{ "median": { "firstView": {
  "requests": { "min": 10, "max": 30 }
}}}
```

Setting Default Operations and Labels

It is possible to optionally define default operations and label templates inside the defaults property in the specs JSON file:

```
{
  "defaults": {
    "suiteName": "Performance Test Suite for example.com",
    "text": ": {actual} should be {operation} {expected} for {metric}",
    "operation": ">"
  },
  "median": { "firstView": {
    "score_gzip": 80,
    "score_keep-alive": 80
  }}
}
```

The test suite name and specs text label templates will be used in lieu of the prede-fined default ones. Using the previous test spec file should output:

```
Performance Test Suite for example.com
    1) 70 should be greater than 80 for median.firstView.score_gzip
    ✓ 100 should be greater than 80 for median.firstView.score_keep-alive

1 passing (3 ms)
1 failing
```

If the defaults property is omitted, the following properties are used:

```
"defaults": {
  "suiteName": "WebPageTest",
  "text": "{metric}: {actual} should be {operation} {expected}",
  "operation": "<"
}
```

Available Output Text Template Tags

{metric}
> metric name—for example, median.firstView.loadTime

{actual}
> The value returned from the actual test results—for example, 300

{operation}
> The long operation name—for example, less than

{expected}
> The defined expected value—for example, 200

Available Assertion Operations

<

Less than

>

Greater than

<>

Greater than and less than (range)

=

Equal to

Overriding Labels

Overriding individual spec labels is also possible by providing `text` in the spec object:

```
{ "median": { "firstView": {
  "loadTime": {
    "text": "page load time took {actual}ms and should be no more
      than {expected}ms",
    "max": 3000
  }
}}}
```

Which outputs:

```
WebPageTest
    ✓ page load time took 2500ms and should be no more than 3000ms

1 passing (2 ms)
```

Specifying Test Reporter

The WebPageTest API Wrapper test specs use Mocha (*http://visionmedia.github.io/mocha*) to build and run a test suite. Once a test suite is done, a reporter formats and builds the output results. The following reporters are available:

- dot (default)
- spec
- tap
- xunit
- list
- progress

- min

- nyan

- landing

- json

- doc

- markdown

- teamcity

Test Specs Examples

Asserting the results of a WebPageTest test varies because it depends on the key performance metrics you are measuring for your pages. The WebPageTest API Wrapper test specs provide several ways to assert any metric provided by the WebPageTest API. Following are some examples that you can adapt to your particular case.

Asserting by MIME type

By either running tests synchronously or just fetching results, it is possible to test by MIME type:

```
{
  "median": {
    "firstView": {
      "breakdown": {
        "js": {
          "requests": 6,
          "bytes": 200000
        },
        "css": {
          "requests": 1,
          "bytes": 50000
        },
        "image": {
          "requests": 10,
          "bytes": 300000
        }
      }
    }
  }
}
```

The preceding spec only allows up to 6 JavaScript requests summing up to 200 KB, 1 CSS request up to 50 KB, and no more than 10 images up to 300 KB total.

Asserting by processing breakdown

When runnning tests synchronously in Chrome with the `--timeline` option, it is possible to test by processing breakdown:

```
{
  "run": {
    "firstView": {
      "processing": {
        "RecalculateStyles": 1300,
        "Layout": 2000,
        "Paint": 800
      }
    }
  }
}
```

The preceding spec only allows up to 1,300 ms of recalculate styles, 2,000 ms of layout, and 800 ms of paint time processing. Thus, it avoids rendering regression once these metrics are known by measuring multiple times from previous tests.

Jenkins Integration

You can integrate the WebPageTest API Wrapper with Jenkins (*https://jenkins-ci.org*) and other CI tools seamlessly. To do so, run commands to test synchronously with either `--poll` or `--wait` (if the Jenkins server is reachable from a private instance of the WebPageTest server), and specify a `--specs` file or JSON string with either `tap` or `xunit` as `--reporter`.

Configuring Jenkins

Jenkins expects the output of a test suite result in a known format so it can parse individual results and alert in case tests are not passing the expected results. Here are a couple of the most common reporters supported by Jenkins:

Using TAP as test resporter

The *Test Anything Protocol* (TAP) is a plug-in that can be installed via the Jenkins Plugin Manager. Assuming *example.com* has the following configuration:

- Staging server: *staging.corp.example.com*
- Jenkins server: *jenkins.corp.example.com*
- WebPageTest private instance: *wpt.corp.example.com*
- WebPageTest location named `Default` with Chrome browser
- Jenkins has a */specs* directory with test specs JSON files, with:

/specs/homepage.json:

```
{
  "median": {
    "firstView": {
      "requests": 20,
      "render": 400,
      "loadTime": 3000,
      "score_gzip": {
        "min": 90
      }
    }
  }
}
```

The build shell command to be executed is:

```
webpagetest test http://staging.corp.example.com \
--server http://wpt.corp.example.com --first --location Default:Chrome \
--wait jenkins.corp.example.com:8000 --specs /specs/homepage.json \
--reporter tap > homepage.tap
```

Jenkins (the tool) has a "Post-build Actions" section where users should input `home page.tap` as "Test results." You can see a screenshot at *http://bit.ly/wpt-jenkins*.

Using JUnit as a test reporter

Using the same TAP example but without plug-ins, Jenkins can report JUnit by default with the following build shell command:

```
webpagetest test http://staging.corp.example.com \
--server http://wpt.corp.example.com --first --location Default:Chrome \
--wait jenkins.corp.example.com:8000 --specs /specs/homepage.json \
--reporter xunit > homepage.xml
```

Jenkins postbuild actions should publish a JUnit test result report for *homepage.xml*.

Travis-CI Integration

Similar to Jenkins integration, Travis-CI (*https://travis-ci.org*) also requires that tests should be run synchronously via the `--poll` option, as it's very unlikely that Travis-CI workers are reachable from private or public instances of WebPageTest servers. `--specs` is required to test the results, but `--reporter` is not as important, because Travis-CI relies on the exit status rather than the output format as like Jenkins does.

Configuring Travis-CI

The following is an example of a WebPageTest performance test for a contrived Node project in a GitHub public repo. Add a test script to the *package.json* file:

```
{
  "name": "example",
  "version": "0.0.1",
  "dependencies": {
    "webpagetest": ""
  },
  "scripts": {
    "test": "./node_modules/webpagetest/bin/webpagetest
            test http://staging.example.com
            --server http://webpagetest.example.com
            --key $WPT_API_KEY
            --first
            --location MYVM:Chrome
            --poll
            --timeout 60
            --specs specs.json
            --reporter spec"
  }
}
```

Note that line breaks were added to the test script for clarity; it should be in a single line.

This test script will:

1. Schedule a test on a private instance of WebPageTest hosted on *http://webpagetest.example.com*, which must be publicly reachable from Travis-CI workers

2. Use a WebPageTest API key from `WPT_API_KEY` (environment variable, see "Encrypting the WebPageTest API key" on page 128)

3. Test *http://staging.example.com*, which must be publicly reachable from WebPageTest agents

4. Run a test for first view only

5. Run from location MYVM on Chrome browser

6. Poll results every five seconds (default)

7. Time out in 60 seconds if no results are available

8. Test the results against the *specs.json* spec file

9. Output using the spec reporter

Encrypting the WebPageTest API key

If you are scheduling your tests to run from public instances of Travis-CI workers, such as from a public GitHub repository, WebPageTest API keys (`--key` or `-k`) should be used to prevent abuse, but *do not* put unencrypted API keys in public files. Fortunately, Travis-CI provides an easy way to do this via secure environment variables (*http://docs.travis-ci.com/user/environment-variables*), which avoid explicitly passing $WPT_API_KEY in the public *.travis.yml* file.

Install Travis and go to the repo directory:

```
gem install travis
...
cd repo_dir
```

Next, encrypt the WebPageTest API key as a secure environment variable:

```
travis encrypt WPT_API_KEY=super_secret_api_key_here --add
```

Note that it must run from the repo directory or use -r or --repo to specify the repo name in the format user/repo—for example, marcelduran/webpagetest-api.

By default, the --add flag will append the encrypted string to the *.travis.yml* file as:

```
env:
  global:
    - secure: +_\encrypted WPT_API_KEY=super_secret_api_key_here string\_+
```

In this chapter, we covered how the WebPageTest API can be integrated into your web development pipeline via CI. It helps you leverage the quality of your web pages by preventing key performance metrics from regressing during push cycles. It can also help you track some performance metrics values over time so you can measure the impact of adding new features to the page. Once WebPageTest is integrated into your CI tool, after several pushing cycles you start getting a better idea of the state of perfomance of your pages. Data collected from CI can be used to plot historical information about your pages' performance. It can catch unexpected regressions in non–performance-related expected changes. Some metrics can be easy to track and catch, such as the number of requests, but some, especially those related to time, can require some tuning to find an optimum range.

CHAPTER 11

Private Instances

In Chapter 9, we discussed how to use WebPageTest's API to submit tests, check their status, and retrieve the results.

Using the public API is a great way to get started with the API, but the number of tests you can run is limited to around 200 per day.

 WebPageTest counts every first view and every repeat view as separate tests; scripted tests that involve more than one page currently count as a single test, but that's likely to change in the future.

Once you start to automate testing, you'll probably find that you want to test more pages more frequently. For example, you might want to measure how a site changes over time or test each build in a continuous integration process. Once you start testing frequently, a usage limit of 200 tests per day doesn't stretch far.

The public site is shared among all users, and API tests run at a lower priority than tests submitted via the Web, so if many other people are testing at the location you want to use, you may have to wait for a while.

 Dulles generally has more than one test agent for each browser, but most other locations only have a single agent that is often shared among all browsers.

There's also the challenge that *webpagetest.org* can only test publicly accessible URLs, so if the site you want to test is behind a firewall, you may be out of luck! Of course you could poke holes in your firewall or use a proxy service to reach sites behind a firewall, but the proxy service is likely to affect timings.

Finally, it's also worth mentioning that although you can mark tests as private, they are still accessible to anyone who has (or can discover) the test URL. Fortunately, it's possible to use your own instance of WebPageTest to overcome these challenges. In this chapter, we'll look at how to install it, what the options for test agents are, and how to keep it up and running smoothly.

We'll also discuss some of the features, such as bulk tests, that are only available in a private instance.

How Does WebPageTest Work?

Each WebPageTest instance is made up of two types of components: a server and the test agents.

A server provides the web interface and API; it also queues and schedules the work for the individual test agents. After the agents have completed a test, it recieves the results and displays them.

The second type of component is the test agents, which actually load the page in a browser and gather metrics as it loads. These test agents might be desktop browsers running on Windows, Safari running on a iOS device, Android devices running Chrome, or remote ones on another WebPageTest instance.

The test agents poll the server for work, measure the page load, and then when the test completes, upload the measurements and any screenshots it took (Figure 11-1).

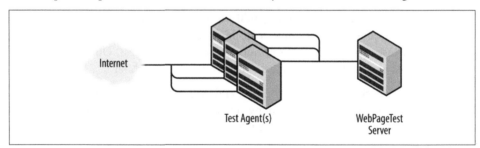

Figure 11-1. Test agents polling the WebPageTest server

Windows test agents are the most mature and fully featured; they can be scripted and are relatively easy to support. The Android mobile agents capture a greater level of detail than the iOS ones, but neither supports full scripting yet. Both of these mobile agents are based on closed platforms, which imposes some limitations as well.

We'll start by using the preconfigured Amazon Machine Images (AMIs) and then walk through installing our own instance from scratch with some desktop test agents. Then we'll add mobile and other test agents to our setup.

Using the Preconfigured AWS AMI

The simplest and fastest way to get WebPageTest up and running is to use the preconfigured Amazon Web Services (AWS) AMIs.

There are server AMIs available for each AWS region, and they come preconfigured to launch test agents in all the AWS locations on demand (to reduce costs, they also shut down test agents when they've been idle for a while).

To start, you'll need an AWS account, a user with the permissions to manage EC2 instances, and Amazon Simple Storage Service (S3) (if you want to archive tests to S3).

Create an AWS User with Relevant Permissions

In the AWS console, create a new user in Security Credentials → Users → Create New Users and give the user an appropriate name, such as WPT.

When creating the user, remember to tick the box to "Generate an access key for each user," and then save the Access Key ID and Secret Access Key that were generated, as you'll need to provide these as part of the instance configuration.

Once the user has been created, it needs permissions to manage EC2 instances and for S3 storage to archive older tests.

In the AWS console, create two groups; in this example, they're named WPT-EC2 and WPT-S3.

Each can be granted all permissions for the service (e.g., `ec2:*` and `s3:*`), or for finer-grained permissions, use the permissions listed here:

```
WPT-EC2

ec2:CreateTags
ec2:DescribeRegions
ec2:DescribeVolumes
ec2:DeleteVolume
ec2:DescribeInstances
ec2:RunInstances
ec2:StartInstances
ec2:StopInstances
ec2:TerminateInstances
```

```
WPT-S3

s3:GetObject
s3:PutObject
```

Once the groups have been created, add the WPT user to them so that it has the necessary permissions to manage EC2 instances and S3 storage.

Configure and Launch the AWS Instance

You can find a list of the latest versions of the AMI (*https://github.com/WPO-Foundation/webpagetest/blob/master/docs/EC2/Server%20AMI.md*) on a per-region basis in the WebPageTest GitHub repository.

In the EC2 Dashboard, choose Launch Instance and then search the Community AMIs for the WebPageTest server AMI. Select the one you want and choose an appropriate instance size; t2.micro is an easy one to start with for the server.

In the next step, Configure Instance Details, scroll down to the bottom of the page and open the Advanced Details Panel. This is where the User Data for the instance is specified—for example, the user keys we created earlier and the WebPageTest settings we want to apply.

The `ec2_key` and `ec2_secret` should be assigned the values for the WPT user you created earlier. You can choose any value you want for the `api_key`; it's just the value you need to pass when submitting a test.

```
ec2_key=Access Key ID
ec2_secret=Secret Access Key
api_key=your-api-key
```

By default, the server runs in headless mode, and tests can only be submitted via the API. If you want to enable the normal web interface for submitting tests, add `head less=0` to the user data.

 If you choose to disable headless mode, you might want to protect the site using HTTP Auth to prevent others from submitting tests.

If you do this, remember to exclude the */var/www/webpagetest/www/work* folder, as it contains the endpoints that the agents use to check for work, submit results, etc., and the test agents don't support accessing the server using HTTP Auth yet.

Remember to update the security group so that both port 22 (SSH) and port 80 (HTTP) are open; otherwise, you won't be able to submit tests and the agents won't be able to poll for work.

Once the instance is up and running, you can visit it in a browser. If the instance is running in headless mode (see the headless home page in Figure 11-2), you'll see the normal familiar WebPageTest interface but without the ability to interactively submit tests.

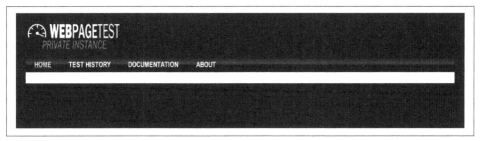

Figure 11-2. Headless instance home page

To check that the install is working, submit a test. You can do this via a browser, `wget`, or a REST client such as Postman (we normally use Postman):

```
http://your-server-ip/runtest.php?f=json&url=http://news.bbc.co.uk&k=your-api-key
```

The server should return a response with a `statusCode` of `200` with contents similar to:

```
{
  "statusCode": 200,
  "statusText": "Ok",
  "data": {
    "testId": "150131_Q0_1",
    "ownerKey": "b9941c6d6336f236287b497a56c4a8f4622a5827",
    "jsonUrl": "http:\/\/your-server-ip\/jsonResult.php?test=150131_Q0_1",
    "xmlUrl": "http:\/\/your-server-ip\/xmlResult\/150131_Q0_1\/",
    "userUrl": "http:\/\/your-server-ip\/result\/150131_Q0_1\/",
    "summaryCSV": "http:\/\/your-server-ip\/result\/150131_Q0_1\/page_data.csv",
    "detailCSV": "http:\/\/your-server-ip\/result\/150131_Q0_1\/requests.csv"
  }
}
```

The job is now queued, and WebPageTest will spin up an agent on an EC2 instance to run the test.

You can see the job waiting for an agent to become available via `/getLocations.php`.

If you watch in the EC2 Dashboard, you will also see the instance for the test agent starting up. If you've used a test location that's in another AWS region, you'll need to switch AWS regions in the dashboard to see this.

Once the test has completed, its results can be retrieved via `jsonURL` or `xmlURL` specified in the original response, or the waterfall and other test details can be viewed via `userUrl`.

To reduce costs, the test agent will shut down after about an hour unless it receives any work in the last 15 minutes of the hour.

Even though the agent will shut down when it's been idle for a while, /getLoca tions.php and /getTesters.php will both show a tester is available after the EC2 instance has shut down.

The server AMI comes preconfigured with test agents in all the AWS regions. You can see the full list of agent locations via /getLocations.php.

Creating Your Own Local Installation

If you don't want to use AWS to host your WebPageTest instance, then you can install it on your own local hardware and run either local or remote test agents.

The server application is a straightforward PHP application and will run on Windows, Linux, or Mac OS X.

We tend to install the server into *c:\wpt-www* on Windows, or a *wpt* folder under the web server's document root on Mac OS X and Linux.

First we'll start by configuring Apache and PHP, and then we'll add the WebPageTest files:

1. In Apache's configuration, ensure that the expires, headers, and rewrite modules are enabled and that PHP is installed and enabled, too.

2. WebPageTest depends on GD2, ImageMagick, ffmpeg, jpegtran, and exiftool, so install these as well.

3. Update the following entries in *php.ini* to match the values shown here:

   ```
   upload_max_filesize = 10M
   post_max_size = 10M
   memory_limit = 256M
   ```

   Once the base server is configured, we can install the WebPageTest server components.

4. Download the latest private release of WebPageTest (*https://github.com/WPO-Foundation/webpagetest/releases*) from GitHub and extract the contents of the *www* folder into the folder you're going to use.

   The configuration files for WebPageTest are an *.ini* format and stored in the *settings* folder.

5. Copy *settings/settings.ini.sample* to *settings/settings.ini*.

6. Copy *settings/connectivity.ini.sample* to *settings/connectivity.ini*.

7. WebPageTest needs to store results, queues of work in progress, etc., so we need to give the web-server user write privileges to the following folders:

```
tmp
results
work/jobs
work/video
logs
```

8. Restart Apache.

WebPageTest comes with a handy script that checks many of its dependencies, and we can use this to verify our configuration so far.

9. In a browser, open *http://your-webpagetest-server/install*, and hopefully you'll be greeted by a screen showing that all the mandatory dependencies are installed OK (Figure 11-3).

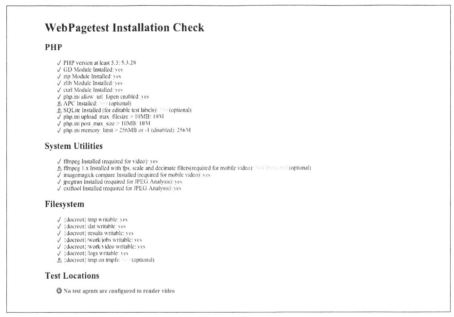

Figure 11-3. Install checker

10. If all is configured correctly, loading the WebPageTest home page should look like Figure 11-4.

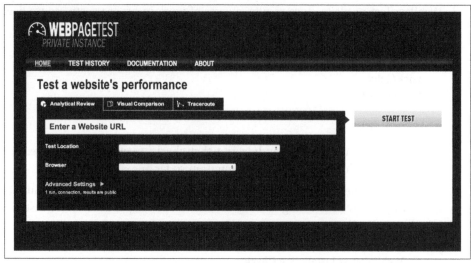

Figure 11-4. Private instance home page

As we haven't configured any test locations yet, the Test Location and Browser drop-downs are still blank; adding test agents is our next step.

Desktop Test Agents

The desktop test agents are Windows-based; both 32-bit and 64-bit versions of Windows 7, 8, and Server 2012 can all be used as hosts. Windows XP will also work, but because it's reached End of Life, we won't cover it here.

Machine size is one of the key factors in getting consistent, representative test results. Test agents can be run on either hardware or virtual machines. We normally use virtual machines with 2 vCPUs and 2 GB of RAM running on a quad core i7 host.

 If you don't own any Windows licenses and want to experiment with desktop test agents, you can either download a virtual machine image from *http://modern.ie* or use a one of the preconfigured Amazon EC2 AMIs.

In this example, we'll configure one location with a Windows 7 test agent that's running Chrome, Firefox, and Internet Explorer 11:

1. Install some form of antivirus software such as Microsoft Security Essentials.

2. Install Chrome and Firefox.

3. Disable User Account Control.

In the search box, type UAC, click on Change User Account Control settings, and then slide the slider to Never Notify.

4. If you're running Windows in a virtual machine, force it to use the platform clock using BCDedit from an administrative shell:

`bcdedit /set {default} useplatformclock true`

5. Configure Windows to always log in using an account that has local administration rights:

   a. Click Start and launch netplwiz.

   b. In the User Accounts dialog box, select the account you want to automatically log on and uncheck the Users Must Enter A User Name And Password To Use This Computer checkbox.

   c. Click OK and, in the Automatically Log On dialog, enter the user's password twice and click OK.

When Windows is restarted, it will now automatically log on with the selected account.

1. To save power, Windows will by default turn the display off and go to sleep after set periods of time. The power settings need to be changed to prevent this:

   a. In Control Panel, choose System and Security → Power Options, and create a new Power Plan called Never Off.

   b. Turn off the display Never.

   c. Put the display to sleep Never.

   d. In Advanced settings, change Require a password on wakeup to No.

Now that the base Windows image is configured, we can install the WebPageTest agent software:

1. Extract the agent folder from the *webpagetest_x.xx.zip* file into *c:\wpt-agent*.

2. Install DummyNet.

   The desktop agents use DummyNet to shape the network connection during tests, and both 32-bit and 64-bit versions of DummyNet are shipped in the WebPageTest ZIP file.

   Depending on your platform, choose the version of DummyNet you need and copy the contents of the 32-bit or 64-bit folder into *c:\wpt-agent\dummynet*.

   In the properties of the Network Adapter used for Internet access:

   a. Click Install.

   b. Select Service and click Add.

c. Click Have Disk and navigate to *c:\wpt-agent\dummynet*.

d. Select the *ipfw+dummynet* service (and click through any warnings about the driver being unsigned).

   If you're connected via Remote Desktop, you'll probably lose the connection while installing DummyNet and need to reconnect after.

   Now we need to configure WPTDriver via its *ini* file:

```
[WebPageTest]
url=http://your-webpagetest-server
location=Local-WPTDriver ❶
browser=chrome
Time Limit=120
;Automatically install and update support software (Flash, Silverlight, etc)
software=http://your-webpagetest-server/installers/software.dat

[Chrome] ❷
exe="C:\Program Files (x86)\Google\Chrome\Application\chrome.exe"
options='--load-extension="%WPTDIR%\extension" --user-data-dir="%PROFILE%" --no-proxy-se
installer=http://your-webpagetest-server/installers/browsers/chrome.dat

[Firefox] ❷
exe="C:\Program Files (x86)\Mozilla Firefox\firefox.exe"
options='-profile "%PROFILE%" -no-remote'
installer=http://your-webpagetest-server/installers/browsers/firefox.dat
template=firefox

[IE11] ❷
exe="C:\Program Files\Internet Explorer\iexplore.exe"
```

❶ Location name must match one of the locations in *settings/location.ini* on the server.

❷ The browser sections must also match the browsers configured under the location in *locations.ini*.

At this stage, it's worth rechecking that the paths to the individual browsers are correct because, depending on whether you're running a 32-bit or 64-bit version of Windows, Chrome, or Firefox, they will be in different locations. For a 32-bit version of Windows, they will be in *Program Files*; on a 64-bit operating system, they'll be in *Program Files x86)*.

Now create a shortcut to *c:\wpt-agent\wptdriver.exe* in the startup folder.

Originally, WebPageTest used *urlblast.exe* to drive Internet Explorer, and *wptdriver.exe* for Chrome and Firefox.

As WPTDriver can now drive Internet Explorer, and URLBlast is likely to be deprecated soon, we've skipped installing it here.

If you want to learn more about URLBlast, it's still covered by the WebPageTest documentation and it has some features that are yet to be ported to WPTDriver.

Finally, we need to clear the default browser and other security prompts:

1. Launch each browser and clear the prompts such as requests to be the default browser, whether extensions should be loaded, etc.

2. From the startup folder, launch WPTDriver and ipfw.cmd manually. Give each of them permission to run even though they're unsigned, and uncheck the "always do this" box.

3. Now restart the test agent; it should start polling the server for work. If it's polling for work successfully, there will be requests for `/work/getwork.php` in the Apache logs.

If you access the test agent via Remote Desktop, you must restart it when you finish; otherwise, the desktop will be locked and screen captures will fail.

When accessed via Remote Desktop, Windows 7 doesn't display the Restart option on the Start Menu. You can create a desktop shortcut by **shutdown -f -r -t 1**, so you've got that option.

Now that a test agent is configured, we need to configure the server so that we can submit tests for it, and this is done via *settings/locations.ini* on the server.

Locations.ini has a hierarchical structure of:

```
Location -> Agents at each location -> Browsers at each location
```

There's already a *locations.ini.sample* in the *settings* folder, so we could rename and edit this, but instead we're going to start with our own simple version and update it as we add more agents.

In the settings folder on the server, create a file called *locations.ini* with the following contents:

```
[locations] ❶
1=Local
default=Local

[Local] ❷
1=Local-WPTDriver
label="Local"

[Local-WPTDriver] ❸
browser=Chrome,Firefox,IE11
label="local"
```

❶ List of configured test locations, which matches the location drop-down in the WebPageTest interface.

❷ List of test agents configured for each location; there will be one of these sections for each location.

❸ Individual test agent details; in this example, the test agent has Chrome, Firefox, and Internet Explorer 11 installed.

This tells our WebPageTest install that we have one location with a single test agent running Chrome, Firefox, and Internet Explorer 11.

We've started with a simple configuration, but later in the chapter we'll add more locations and test agents.

Now that we've configured both the test agent and the server, we can run our first test to make sure everything works as expected:

1. Restart Apache, and then load your instance of WebPageTest in a browser and submit a test.

2. Hopefully you'll see a successful test result, but if you don't take a look at "Troubleshooting" on page 159 later in this chapter.

3. Once you've run the first test, edit *settings.ini* to increase the number of *maxRuns* allowed (we often use 49), then test some well-known stable pages, such as BBC News, Google, etc., for a large number of runs and make sure that the test agents are producing consistent results. (Remember to change the setting back if you want to limit how may test runs someone can submit.)

As an alternative to hosting your own test agents, there are also preconfigured AMIs. They're listed in the WebPageTest documentation (*https://sites.google.com/a/webpagetest.org/docs/private-instances#TOC-EC2-Test-Agents*) and are easy to setup.

Once your instance is up and running, if you find it's getting busy and you're having to wait too long for jobs to complete, you can set up multiple test-agent machines with the same location name to share the workload.

Mobile Test Agents

So far we've covered installing desktop agents, but more and more people are accessing our sites using phones, tablets, and other mobile devices.

WebPageTest supports both Chrome and Chrome Beta on Android, and Safari on iOS. The Android test agents provide a greater level of detail and have more features than the iOS agents; for example, the iOS agent only provides overall request and response times for each request rather than breaking out the separate timings for DNS lookup, TCP connect, and SSL negotiation.

 Configuring the mobile agents involves voiding the warranty on the devices, so you might want to use secondhand devices.

The mobile agents connect to the WebPageTest server via a Node.js application. The Node application polls the server for work, drives the test device to load the page, and then returns the results to the server. This process is depicted in Figure 11-5.

The Node.js application and the browser communicate using the Chrome Remote Debugging protocol. iOS uses the same protocol wrapped up in binary plists, so we need to use a proxy that translates between the two.

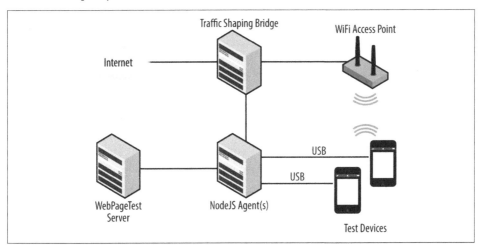

Figure 11-5. Node.js app connecting to the WebPageTest server

Install Agent

The agent that acts as a bridge between the server and the test devices can be installed on any platform that supports Node.js. We've had success on Linux, Windows, and Mac OS X.

1. Install Node.js from *http://nodejs.org/*.

2. There's a *mobile* folder in the release of WebPageTest we used to install the desktop agents. Extract this to a *wpt-mobile* folder.

3. If you're planning on using Android test agents, download and install the Android SDK (*http://developer.android.com/sdk/index.html*), and make sure that the Android Debug Bridge (ADB) is available on the path.

Once the Node.js agent has been installed, we need to configure mobile devices on which to run tests. The Android devices will need their bootloaders unlocked, and the iOS devices will need to be jailbroken, so it might be worth considering buying used devices from eBay, Craigslist, etc.

Add Android Devices

For Android you'll need a phone or tablet running Android 4.4 (KitKat) or later that can be *rooted*.

In this section, we'll use a Moto G and a Nexus 7 as our test devices, but we could also use a Moto E, Nexus 4 or 5, etc.

Install the Android Debug Bridge (ADB)

Download and install the Android SDK (*http://developer.android.com/sdk/index.html*).

Unlock the bootloader

Unlocking the bootloader will wipe all content and installed applications from the device, so be sure to back up anything you want to keep.

We've *bricked* a Moto G while rooting it, and a colleague did the same to a Nexus 7 (both were restored and worked eventually), so it's worth finding out how to restore the device just in case you need to.

Moto G:

1. Motorola provides an official route to unlock the bootloader (*https://motorola-global-portal.custhelp.com/app/standalone/bootloader/unlock-your-device-a/action/auth*).

2. You'll be asked to agree to some terms and conditions and either log in with a Google account or create a Motorola one before being given straightforward instructions on how to unlock the bootloader.

3. Once the bootloader is unlocked, install Superboot (*https://motorola-global-portal.custhelp.com/app/standalone/bootloader/unlock-your-device-a/action/auth*).

4. Launch Superboot and Enable Superuser (root) access. Set the Default Access to Grant, and disable notifications.

Nexus 7:

1. Unlock Bootloader (*http://forum.xda-developers.com/showthread.php?t=2379618*).

2. Root the device by following the Android instructions (*http://www.teaman droid.com/2014/06/20/root-nexus-7-2013-android-444-ktu84p-kitkat-install-cwm/2/*).

Configure Android

Because Android devices need to be associated with a Google account, consider using a separate Gmail account so that you don't need to worry about others having access to your email, tests affecting your search history, etc.

Once the bootloader has been unlocked, we need to configure various Android settings ready for testing:

1. Launch Google Play and configure it to automatically install updates (using the menu in the top-left corner).

2. Launch the Android settings utility.

3. Disable Screen lock by setting it to none in the Security section.

4. If you're going to be using a device only for portrait testing, disable Auto-rotate in the Display section. As an alternative, you could install Adaptive Rotation Lock or one of the other rotation apps from the Play store.

5. Mute all the sounds, including music, ringtone, and alarms, in the Sound section.

6. Enable Airplane mode via More… under Wireless & Networks, and then connect to a WiFi network.

7. Activate developer mode by tapping on the OS Version seven times (it's within the About Phone section).

8. Under Developer options, enable USB debugging, and set the device to always Stay awake.

9. Finally, install Chrome and Chrome Beta from the Play Store, and ensure they're updated to the latest release; then launch both, accept the Terms of Service, and clear any dialogs such as the "Help make Chrome better" one.

Once you've finished configuring the whole device, it's also worth turning down the screen brightness to reduce power usage and heat generated.

Add the agent to the server

To enable the new device to be used for testing, we need to update the server's *locations.ini* as follows:

```
[locations]
1=Local
default=Local

[Local]
1=Local-WPTDriver
2=Local-MotoG    ❶
label="Local"

[Local-WPTDriver]
browser=Chrome,Firefox,IE11
label="local"

[Local-MotoG] ❷
browser=Moto-G - Chrome,Moto-G - Chrome Beta
label="Moto-G"
type=nodejs,mobile
connectivity="WiFi"
```

❶ Adds the test device.

❷ List the device, the browsers that are available, and the bandwidth configuration.

Check that the agent works

Finally, we're now in a position to fire up the Node.js agent and run our first test on the device.

First we need the ID of our test device. At a command prompt, type **adb devices**, accept the permissions dialog that appears on the phone, and you should get a response similar to:

```
List of devices attached
AA737KSVW    device
```

The folder in which the Node.js agent was installed, *wpt-mobile*, contains both a shell script for Linux and Mac OS X, and a batch file for Windows.

Start the agent on Linux or Mac OS X by running the command shown here:

```
./wptdriver.sh \
  -m debug \
  --browser android:AA737KSVW \  ❶
  --serverUrl 127.0.0.1 \  ❷
  --location Local-MotoG  ❸
```

❶   Device ID as retrieved from `adb devices`.

❷   URL of the WebPageTest server.

❸   Name of the location in the servers, *locations.ini*.

Once the agent has started, it should be available via the server's web interface, so you can go and run your first test.

Add iOS Devices

Configuring an iOS test agent is a bit more involved than configuring an Android one due to iOS being even more closed and there being no official support for unlocking the bootloader from Apple (a.k.a, *jailbreaking*).

The tests from iOS give less waterfall detail—they're missing DNS lookup, TCP connect, and TLS negotiation times, but can capture video of the page loading.

To configure an iOS test agent, you'll need a device that runs iOS 8.x or above and has a lightning connection, so that video can be captured. There must also be a jailbreak available, as the host connects via SSH to remove caches and other data between runs.

If you want to capture video of the page loading, the host machine will need to be able to run OS X 10.10 (Yosemite) or above. At present, OS X only supports capturing video from one device at a time, so you'll need an OS X host per device!

You'll need the mobile agent code from v2.19 of WebPageTest, or if v2.19 isn't available, you can pull the code straight from the GitHub repository.

Jailbreak the iOS device

WebPageTest needs iOS devices to be jailbroken so caches and other browser data-stores can be completely cleared during testing.

There are several options for jailbreaking iOS devices that change on a release-by-release basis, so some research will be required to know what version of iOS can be jailbroken.

Enable SSH

Once the device has been jailbroken, install OpenSSH from *Cydia*.

By default, the SSH password will be *alpine,* so as a first step, you need to change this to prevent others from accessing the phone.

You can either connect the device to WiFi and find its IP address to access SSH, or connect via a lightning cable and use TCP Relay. These instructions assume the device is connected via a cable.

`tcprelay` and other python utilities that are needed can be found in *agent/js/lib/ios/ usbmux_python_client.*

1. Change their permissions so that they are executable:

   ```
   chmod +x agent/js/lib/ios/usbmux_python_client/*.py
   ```

2. Launch the relay agent so that you can connect to the device—this maps port 2222 on the host to port 22 on the device:

   ```
   agent/js/lib/ios/usbmux_python_client/tcprelay.py -t 22:2222
   ```

3. In another terminal window, connect to the device:

   ```
   ssh -p 2222 root@localhost
   ```

   The default Apple password should be *alpine,* but check the OpenSSH instructions if you cannot connect.

4. Once connected, change the root password:

   ```
   passwd
   ```

5. You should be prompted for a new password and asked to repeat it.

6. Change the password for the regular user account:

   ```
   passwd mobile
   ```

7. Again, you'll be prompted for the new password and asked to repeat it.

8. Finally, create a folder for SSH keys. These are so the host can use key-based authentication to access the device when it's running tests.

   ```
   mkdir ~/.ssh
   ```

Once the device has been configured for SSH access, you need to generate a public/ private key pair on the host and transfer them across.

1. Change to the .ssh folder:

   ```
   cd ~/.ssh
   ```

   a. Generate the key:

      ```
      ssh-keygen -t dsa
      ```

   b. When prompted for a key name, enter *id_dsa_ios,* and don't protect it with a pass phrase.

2. Now that the key pair has been generated, you need to transfer the public key to the device:

```
scp -P 2222 id_dsa_ios.pub root@localhost:~/.ssh
```

3. Add it to the device's authorized keys file

    a. Connect to the device via SSH (when prompted, enter the password you set previously):

    ```
    ssh -p 2222 -i root@localhost
    ```

    b. Change to the key folder:

    ```
    cd ~/.ssh
    ```

    c. Add the key to the *authorized_key2* folder and set its permissions:

    ```
    cat id_dsa_ios.pub >> authorized_keys2
    chmod 0600 authorized_keys2
    ```

4. To check if SSH is configured correctly, disconnect your SSH session and then reconnect using the following key:

```
ssh -p 2222 -i ~/.ssh/id_dsa_ios root@localhost
```

Update phone settings

Now that SSH has been configured, there's a few device settings that need to be changed.

1. Connect the device to your chosen WiFi network.

2. Switch to airplane mode to disable cellular connections and then enable WiFi so the device can connect to your chosen WiFi network.

3. Enable Web Inspector so that the host can connect to Safari to gather metrics while the page loads:

```
Settings > Safari > Advanced > Web Inspector = ON
```

Now that the device is configured, there's a few more steps to do on the host and server before we can run our first test.

Configure the host

The host application uses Node.js, so ensure it's installed, as in the previous Android steps.

The mobile agent for WebPageTest and other utilities it requires are in the *agent/js* folder, so switch to that folder.

1. Connect the device to the host and ensure that OS X can see it as a web cam by running *xrecord*:

   ```
   lib/ios/video/xrecord --quicktime --list
   ```

   This should list any built-in recording devices on the host, and the device that's connected:

   Available capture devices:

   > AppleHDAEngineInput:1B,0,1,0:1: Built-in Microphone
   >
   > 5f355a5b183b2d2d7ba91dcfadd4c14b98504642: iPhone
   >
   > CC2437519T1F6VVDH: FaceTime HD Camera

2. Once you're sure the device is connected, you need to get the UDID of the device. You can do this via iTunes.

   a. Click on the device, and then in the *Summary*, click on the *Serial Number* to show the UDID.

   b. The UDID will be a long hexdecimal string (for example, cbea881cedf361982433b97a4ead38e8e2b4c3e9), and you can right click to copy it.

   c. Launch the agent using the following command, replacing the UDID of the device, WebPageTest server URL, and location, as appropriate for your configuration:

   ```
   ./wptdriver.sh \
   --browser ios:UDID of device \
   --serverUrl your-webpagetest-server \
   --location Local-iPhone5C
   ```

   The agent will start polling the server for work, but as the server doesn't yet know about the agent then there won't be any work for it to do!

3. In the same way we added the Android agent to *locations.ini* on the server, we need to add the iOS device too:

   ```
   [locations]
   1=Local
   default=Local

   [Local]
   1=Local-WPTDriver
   2=Local-MotoG
   3=Local-iPhone
   label="Local"

   [Local-WPTDriver]
   browser=Chrome,Firefox,IE11
   ```

```
label="local"

[Local-MotoG]
browser=Moto-G - Chrome,Moto-G - Chrome Beta
label="Moto-G"
type=nodejs,mobile
connectivity="WiFi"

[Local-MotoG]
browser=Safari
label="iOS Safari"
type=nodejs,mobile
connectivity="WiFi"
```

4. Now, restart the webserver and the iOS device should be available as a location. Submit a test and check that it works.

Bandwidth Shaping

The Windows test agents use DummyNet to shape the network connection, but throttling the network connection for the mobile devices isn't quite as simple.

The public instance of WebPageTest uses a FreeBSD machine with a wireless access point connected to it as a network gateway for the mobile devices.

On the gateway, there are a set of DummyNet pips for each mobile device that can be individually configured. Originally, all devices were fixed to the same network characteristics, but the Node.js agent that controls each device can connect to the gateway to alter the settings for each test.

WanEm, a network emulator built by Tata, might offer an easier way to get running as an alternative to FreeBSD. The team at Interatec experimented with WanEm, but eventually chose an alternative.

Other options for shaping the network include using a wireless access point that can throttle the network for each device, or a Network Link Conditioner could be configured on each iOS device. These options are simpler to set up but don't offer the same power and flexibility as FreeBSD or WanEm.

Remote Test Agents

We're not limited to the test agents we own and control; we can also configure our instance to use test agents on other WebPageTest instances.

The test is submitted to our local instance and then passed to the test agent with the other WebPageTest instance acting as a relay.

This architecture gives us the ability to extend our own private instances with test agents from other WebPageTest instances (e.g., add some of the public locations as agents in our own private instance).

It also allows us to operate WebPageTest behind the firewall but with agents hosted on the public Internet. For example, you could have test agents and a headless server running on AWS (or similar services) but the main WebPageTest install (with all the test data) locally within the firewall.

In the example *locations.ini* that follows, the Dublin test agent from the public version of WebPageTest has been added:

```
[locations]
1=Local
2=Dublin
default=Local

[Local]
1=Local-WPTDriver
label="Local"

[Dublin]
1=WPT-Dublin
label="Dublin"

[Local-WPTDriver]
browser=Chrome,Firefox,IE11
label="Local-WPTDriver"

[WPT-Dublin] ❶
browser=Chrome,Firefox ❸
label="WPT-Dublin"
relayServer="http://www.webpagetest.org/" ❷
relayKey=Your API Key ❷
relayLocation=ec2-eu-west-1 ❸
```

❶ The WPT-Dublin section configures the remote agent, and the relay entries provide the information needed to pass the test to the remote server.

❷ relayServer is self-explanatory, and relayKey is only needed if the remote server requires a key to use its API.

❸ If you don't already know them—i.e., the other instance owner has given them to you—relayLocation and browser are slightly more involved to figure out.

The easiest way to work them out is to use /getLocations.php, which shows all the locations and test agents attached to an instance, along with their work queues.

Looking at *http://webpagetest.org/getLocations.php*, four locations are listed for Dublin:

```
ec2-eu-west-1:Chrome
ec2-eu-west-1:IE 11
ec2-eu-west-1:Firefox
ec2-eu-west-1:Safari
```

The WPTDriver locations are named as a `location:browser name` pair, so `relayLocation` needs to be set to the matching location and each browser name added to the list in the browser entry in the *.ini* file.

If you configure a browser that doesn't exist at a location, you'll see *Test Error: Invalid Browser Selected:* followed by the browser on the results page for any test that attempts to use it.

 Some public locations are still using URLBlast to drive Internet Explorer, so you will also see locations such as `Miami_IE8`. As URL-Blast becomes less frequently used, this format of location name will get less frequent.

Private-Instance-Only Features

WebPageTest has some features that are only available or can only be preconfigured for tests on private instances.

Bulk Test

In the public version of WebPageTest we can only test one URL at a time. If we want to test a series, we have to submit a test for each.

Private instances have a bulk test feature that allows multiple URLs to be tested using the same set of test parameters, producing aggregate statistics (Figure 11-6).

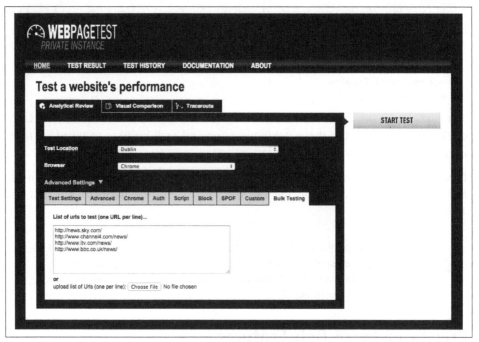

Figure 11-6. WebPageTest private instance bulk testing

Once a set of URLs is inserted in the bulk test field and the test is submitted, the bulk test and its individual tests appear in the list of test results.

Within the bulk test results, you can download both the individual test results and agreggate statistics for all tests (Figure 11-7).

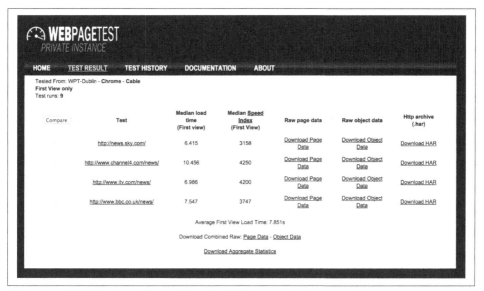

Figure 11-7. Bulk test results are downloadable

Custom Metrics

WebPageTest supports custom metrics, and on the public instance these are defined in the Custom tab for each test.

In a private instance, it's possible to define a set of custom metrics that are generated for every test. Each metric is defined as a JavaScript snippet that returns a single value, and there are several examples already in *settings/custom_metrics*.

To add a new custom metric, create a JavaScript file (e.g., *navtiming.js*) in *settings/ custom_metrics* that calculates and returns the value for the metric.

In this case, *navtiming.js* queries the Navigation Timing API values for the page and returns them as a JSON string so we can return more than one value from the function.

```
return JSON.stringify(window.performance.timing);
```

For each page tested, the script will execute and return the Navigation Timing API values.

You can access the custom metrics via the link in the top-right corner of each view within the test and via the API as well.

Day-to-Day Management

Once you've set up your own WebPageTest instance, it should run fairly trouble-free (most issues we see are related to the initial install and configuration), but there are some maintenance tasks you can do and some other things to be aware of.

Monitoring Queues and Test Agents

Once you have a working WebPageTest instance, others in your team or company will start to use it, and as the instance gets busier, you might find that you need to wait longer for jobs to complete.

WebPageTest provides a few ways to get an understanding of how healthy and busy it is.

Using /getLocations.php you can see each location-browser pair, along with details on how many jobs are waiting in each of its queues. By default, web-submitted jobs have the highest priority and API ones are lower (the actual priority of an API job can be set as a parameter when the test is submitted, but the API key will have a cap on the priority, too).

In Figure 11-8, there are two relay locations, WPT-Dublin and Dulles-Thinkpad, where the local server has been configured to run jobs on another WebPageTest instance, and as /getLocations is unable to report their queue lengths, the information is missing.

Location ID	Description	Idle Testers	Total Tests	Being Tested	High Priority	P1	P2	P3	P4	P5	P6	P7	P8	P9
Local-WPTDriver:Chrome	Local-WPTDriver - Chrome	1	0	0	0	0	0	0	0	0	0	0	0	0
Local-WPTDriver:Firefox	Local-WPTDriver - Firefox	1	0	0	0	0	0	0	0	0	0	0	0	0
Local-WPTDriver:IE11	Local-WPTDriver - IE11	1	0	0	0	0	0	0	0	0	0	0	0	0
WPT-Dublin:Chrome	WPT-Dublin - Chrome													
WPT-Dublin:Firefox	WPT-Dublin - Firefox													
Dulles-Thinkpad:Chrome	Dulles-Thinkpad - Chrome													
Dulles-Thinkpad:Firefox	Dulles-Thinkpad - Firefox													

WebPagetest Admin   Locations   Testers   Usage   Check URLs   Check IPs

Figure 11-8. The Locations tab is unable to report the two locations' queue lengths

/getTesters.php allows you to check whether a test agent is up and whether it's polling for work (Figure 11-9).

WebPagetest Admin   Locations   Testers   Usage   Check URLs   Check IPs

Local-WPTDriver (0 minutes)

Tester	Busy?	Last Check (minutes)	Last Work (minutes)	Version	PC	EC2 Instance	CPU Utilization	Error Rate	Free Disk (GB)	IE Version	GPU?	IP	DNS Server(s
1	0	0	65408	2.16.0.197	LT06168		44	3	10.898		1	192.168.203.1	8.8.8.8,8

WPT-Dublin

Dulles-Thinkpad

Figure 11-9. Testers tab showing a test agent polling for work

By default, both /getLocations.php and /getTesters.php return their data in XML but can also produce JSON- and HTML-formatted responses using &f=json and &f=html respectively.

If you just want to get an understaning of how busy your instance is, /usage.php lists a summary of the jobs submitted over the last week or so, as shown in Figure 11-10.

WebPagetest Admin   Locations   Testers   Usage   Check URLs   Check IPs

Date	Interactive	API	Total
2015/05/19	0	0	0
2015/05/18	5	0	5
2015/05/17	0	0	0
2015/05/16	0	0	0
2015/05/15	2	0	2
2015/05/14	0	0	0
2015/05/13	1	0	1
2015/05/12	8	0	8
Total	16	0	16

Figure 11-10. The Usage tab gives you a history of submitted jobs over a period of time

In the HTML versions of these pages, there are also links to view the URLs tested and the IP addresses where tests are being submitted from.

Archiving Old Tests

Over time, the results of the tests you run will start to fill up the disk of the WebPageTest server.

Depending on your preference, old tests can be archived locally or to Amazon S3 Storage. This behavior is configured in *settings.ini*. Once the test has been archived, the results, filmstrip, etc. can still be accessed through the web interface and API.

To archive to local storage, set the path where the archives will be stored using the `archive_dir` setting.

If you prefer to archive to S3 storage (or a service that conforms to the S3 API), you'll need to set the following entries in *settings.ini*:

```
archive_s3_server=s3.amazonaws.com
archive_s3_key=_access key_
archive_s3_secret=_secret_
archive_s3_bucket=_bucket_
archive_s3_url=http://s3.amazonaws.com/
```

Finally, we need to configure how long the server should wait before archiving old tests:

```
archive_days=7
```

Finally, we need to configure cron or task manager to run the archiving script *www/cli/archive.php* on a regular basis.

On Linux, edit crontab using `crontab -e` and add the following line:

```
0 0 * * * /usr/bin/php /var/www/webpagetest/www/cli/archive.php
```

Ensure that the path to the PHP executable and script are correct. Also check that the script is executable.

Now, every day at midnight all tests that are older than seven days will be archived.

Updating an Instance

New versions of WebPageTest get released a few times a year, and updating your own instance is relatively straightforward:

1. Extract the ZIP file of the new release and then copy the new *www* folder on top of your existing *www* folder. (When Windows agents poll for work, they also check for updates automatically, will download the update from */www/work/update*, and install it on the agent machine.)

2. Update the Node.js agents by copying the contents of the *mobile* folder over the existing install.

Troubleshooting

If your installation isn't working as you expect, there are a few common troubleshooting techniques that you can try.

Check that the test agents are polling for work

Test agents sometimes stop working, and one of the quickest ways to check them is by using /getTesters.php, which allows you to see when they last requested a job from the server.

You can also check that the test agents are polling for work by inspecting the web server logs. Each test agent will make a call to /work/getwork.php, and the value for the location field must match one of the locations in *locations.ini*:

```
192.168.0.10 - - [06/Apr/2015:02:18:40 -0700] "GET /work/getwork.php? \
  shards=1&reboot=1&location=Local-WPTDriver&software=wpt&version= \
   2.16.0.197&ver=197&pc=IE11WIN7&dns=8.8.8.8-8.8.4.4&freedisk= \
    7.718&GPU=0 HTTP/1.1" 200 5 "-" "WebPageTest Driver"
```

If an agent isn't polling for work, check that the server is configured correctly in *wptdriver.ini* or on the Node.js command line.

If the agent appears to be polling for work, try repeating the same request that the agent's making in a browser, using the GET request from the log file as a example.

If the configuration is correct, the response will contain the parameters for a test. For example:

```
Test ID=141016_RE_1
url=http://news.bbc.co.uk
fvonly=1
Capture Video=1
runs=1
bwIn=5000
bwOut=1000
latency=28
plr=0
browser=Chrome
orientation=default
```

On a Windows test agent, check that the agent hasn't gone to sleep; the power settings should be set to keep it always awake.

Watch the test on the device

Depending on the acutal device being used for testing, multiple things can trip up a test. If you're sure the agent is polling for work, it's well worth watching a test run on the actual device.

Typical issues that commonly occur on Windows are:

- Incorrect browser paths in *wptdriver.ini*; remember that browsers have different paths depending on whether they are 32-bit or 64-bit versions of Windows.
- Browser permission dialogs—e.g., extensions requesting permission to execute.
- Screen saver prompting for a password; the screen saver should be configured so that it never prompts for a password.

If the test appears to run OK while you're watching it, then there are a few more things to check:

Check the response from the test agent

When a test completes, the agent POSTs the result data back to the server, so you should see entries for /work/resultimage.php and /work/workdone.php in the web server logs:

```
192.168.0.10 - - [06/Apr/2015:03:04:27 -0700] "POST/work/ \
resultimage.php HTTP/1.1" 200 12 "-" "WebPageTest Driver"
192.168.0.10 - - [06/Apr/2015:03:04:28 -0700] "POST /work/workdone.php \
  HTTP/1.1" 200 5 "-" "WebPageTest Driver"
```

Check the contents of the results folder

WebPageTest stores all the test results in the results folder within its *www* root, and the folder structure is derived from the test ID.

If the URL for a test result was *http://192.168.0.21/result/150406_BH_1/*, the matching folder on disk would be *www/results/15/04/06/BH/1* (15/04/06 is the date in YY/MM/DD format).

In the results folder for a test, there should be a number of files and folders. The exact number and their names will vary depending on the number of test runs and whether repeat views were included in the test.

Typically, the results folder will look something like the excerpt shown here:

```
www/results/15/04/06/BH/1
├── 1.0.visual.dat.gz
├── 1.1.visual.dat.gz
├── 1_Cached_IEWPG.txt.gz
├── 1_Cached_IEWTR.txt.gz
├── 1_Cached_progress.csv.gz
├── 1_Cached_report.txt.gz
├── 1_Cached_screen_doc.jpg
├── 1_Cached_screen.jpg
├── 1_IEWPG.txt.gz
├── 1_IEWTR.txt.gz
├── 1_progress.csv.gz
```

```
├── 1_report.txt.gz
├── 1_screen_doc.jpg
├── 1_screen.jpg
├── video_1
│   ├── frame_0000.hist
│   ├── frame_0000.jpg
│   ├── frame_0105.hist
│   ├── frame_0105.jpg
│   ├── …
│   ├── frame_0138.hist
│   └── frame_0138.jpg
└── video_1_cached
    ├── frame_0000.hist
    ├── frame_0000.jpg
    ├── frame_0013.hist
    ├── frame_0013.jpg
    ├── …
    ├── frame_0022.hist
    └── frame_0022.jpg
```

Check that GD is installed on the server

Blank waterfalls and other images indicate that the GD PHP module isn't installed.

Contributing Changes to WebPageTest

Once you've got your own instance up and running, you're likely to come across things you'd like improved or features you'd like to see included.

One of the great things about WebPageTest is that it's open source, so you can create your own fork on GitHub, make changes, and if appropriate, contribute them. You'll find the root respository at *https://github.com/WPO-Foundation/webpagetest*.

Different parts of the WebPageTest application are written in different languages: the server is mainly PHP, the Windows agents C++, the mobile agents JavaScript, and Python is creeping into the code base, too.

If you're planning on making changes and contributing them, it's well worth talking to Pat Meenan (WebPageTest's creator) first. You can find Pat's contact details on WebPageTest's about page (*http://www.webpagetest.org/about*). Pat's always really helpful, but remember he's got a day job working on Chrome so sometimes he will need time to respond.

When it comes to submitting pull requests (PRs), we've found that atomic requests that are clearly explained get merged more quickly, whereas larger PRs that touch more of the code base take more time to be merged.

If you want some ideas for things you could help improve in WebPageTest, the GitHub issues list is a good place to start, but there's also plenty of room for new features to help people install, troubleshoot, and manage instances.

Running your own private instance of WebPageTest isn't always a trouble-free experience, but it offers a whole range of options that just aren't available with the public version, including adding your own custom network speeds, changing the screenshot size and quality, and more.

In this chapter, we've touched on some of these, but if you explore the configuration files in the settings folder on GitHub you'll discover a whole lot more.

API Input/Output Reference Guide

Examples of Test Results

The following are the verbose output of examples used in Chapter 9.

When Test Is Not Complete

When requesting test results on an unfinished/unstarted test, you may get a partial response:

```
{
  "data": {
    "statusCode": 100,
    "statusText": "Test Started 4 seconds ago",
    "id": "150109_DE_ZW7",
    "testInfo": {
      "url": "http://www.example.com",
      "runs": 1,
      "fvonly": 0,
      "web10": 0,
      "ignoreSSL": 0,
      "label": "",
      "priority": 5,
      "location": "Dulles:Chrome",
      "browser": "Chrome",
      "connectivity": "Cable",
      "bwIn": 5000,
      "bwOut": 1000,
      "latency": 28,
      "plr": "0",
      "tcpdump": 0,
      "timeline": 0,
      "trace": 0,
      "bodies": 0,
```

```
        "netlog": 0,
        "standards": 0,
        "noscript": 0,
        "pngss": 0,
        "iq": 0,
        "keepua": 0,
        "mobile": 0,
        "scripted": 0
    },
    "testId": "150109_DE_ZW7",
    "runs": 1,
    "fvonly": 0,
    "remote": false,
    "testsExpected": 1,
    "location": "Dulles:Chrome",
    "startTime": "01/09/15 17:51:16",
    "elapsed": 4,
    "fvRunsCompleted": 0,
    "rvRunsCompleted": 0,
    "testsCompleted": 0
  },
  "statusCode": 100,
  "statusText": "Test Started 4 seconds ago"
}
```

When Test Is Complete

The following is the complete test results used in the Chapter 9 examples. Some repetitive data is replaced by detailed comments for code readability:

Test result properties may change upon new releases of WebPageTest. Metrics may be added, removed, renamed, or moved. Check WebPageTest releases (*https://github.com/WPO-Foundation/webpagetest/releases*) for more details.

```
{
  "data": {
    "id": "150109_DE_ZW7",
    "url": "http://www.example.com",
    "summary": "http://www.webpagetest.org/results.php?test=150109_DE_ZW7",
    "testUrl": "http://www.example.com",
    "location": "Dulles:Chrome",
    "from": "Dulles, VA - Chrome - <b>Cable</b>",
    "connectivity": "Cable",
    "bwDown": 5000,
    "bwUp": 1000,
    "latency": 28,
    "plr": "0",
    "completed": 1420829496,
    "tester": "IE9203-192.168.102.93",
```

```
"testerDNS": "192.168.102.1",
"runs": {
  "1": {
    "firstView": {
      "URL": "http://www.example.com",
      "loadTime": 194,
      "TTFB": 103,
      "bytesOut": 1548,
      "bytesOutDoc": 344,
      "bytesIn": 86956,
      "bytesInDoc": 1591,
      "connections": 1,
      "requests": [
        // List of details of all requests on tested page. See details below.
      ],
      "requestsDoc": 1,
      "responses_200": 1,
      "responses_404": 1,
      "responses_other": 0,
      "result": 99999,
      "render": 292,
      "fullyLoaded": 271,
      "cached": 0,
      "docTime": 194,
      "domTime": 0,
      "score_cache": 100,
      "score_cdn": -1,
      "score_gzip": -1,
      "score_cookies": -1,
      "score_keep-alive": 100,
      "score_minify": -1,
      "score_combine": 100,
      "score_compress": -1,
      "score_etags": -1,
      "gzip_total": 0,
      "gzip_savings": 0,
      "minify_total": 0,
      "minify_savings": 0,
      "image_total": 0,
      "image_savings": 0,
      "optimization_checked": 1,
      "aft": 0,
      "domElements": 13,
      "pageSpeedVersion": "1.9",
      "title": "Example Domain",
      "titleTime": 290,
      "loadEventStart": 187,
      "loadEventEnd": 190,
      "domContentLoadedEventStart": 187,
      "domContentLoadedEventEnd": 187,
      "lastVisualChange": 0,
      "browser_name": "Google Chrome",
```

```
      "browser_version": "39.0.2171.95",
      "server_count": 1,
      "server_rtt": 31,
      "base_page_cdn": "Edgecast",
      "adult_site": 0,
      "fixed_viewport": 1,
      "score_progressive_jpeg": -1,
      "firstPaint": 251,
      "docCPUms": 140.401,
      "fullyLoadedCPUms": 421.203,
      "docCPUpct": 64,
      "fullyLoadedCPUpct": 13,
      "isResponsive": -1,
      "date": 1420829464,
      "SpeedIndex": 0,
      "visualComplete": 0,
      "run": 1,
      "effectiveBps": 517595,
      "effectiveBpsDoc": 17483,
      "tester": "IE9203-192.168.102.93",
      "pages": {
        // Urls for details, checklist, breakdown, domains, and screenShot.
      },
      "thumbnails": {
        // Urls for waterfall, checklist, and screenShot.
      },
      "images": {
        // Urls for waterfall, connectionView, checklist, and screenShot.
      },
      "rawData": {
        // Urls for headers, pageData, requestsData, and utilization.
      },
      "videoFrames": [
        // List of test video frames objects containing:
        // "time": The time elapsed in _ms_ since test started.
        // "image": The url for video frame image at that time.
        // "VisuallyComplete": The percentage of page (visually) completion.
      ],
      "domains": {
        "www.example.com": {
          "bytes": 1591,
          "requests": 1,
          "connections": 1
        },
        // More domains objects here when mutiple domains available.
      },
      "breakdown": {
        // Total Bytes and number of requests for html, js, css, image,
        //flash, font, and other
      }
    },
    "repeatView": {
```

```
          // Similar to data.runs.1.firstView.
        }
      }
    },
    "fvonly": false,
    "successfulFVRuns": 1,
    "successfulRVRuns": 1,
    "average": {
      "firstView": {
        // Similar to data.runs.1.firstView but without pages, thumbnails,
        // images, rawData, videoFrames, domains, and breakdown.
      },
      "repeatView": {
        // Similar to data.runs.average.firstView.
      }
    },
    "standardDeviation": {
      // Similar to data.runs.average.
    },
    "median": {
      // Similar to data.runs.1.
    }
  },
  "statusCode": 200,
  "statusText": "Test Complete"
}
```

Details of Test Results

The `firstView` and `repeatView` properties from the JSON results previously shown contain all web page performance metrics, described here:

- URL: The tested page URL.

- `loadTime`: The total time taken to load the page (`window.onload`) in ms.

- TTFB: Time to first byte, which is the duration in ms from when the user first made the HTTP request to the very first byte of the page being received by the browser.

- `bytesOut`: The total bytes sent from the browser to other servers.

- `bytesOutDoc`: Same as `bytesOut` but only includes bytes until the Document Complete event. Usually when all the page content has loaded (`window.onload`).

- `bytesIn`: The amount of data that browser had to download in order to load the page. It is also commonly referred to as the page size.

- `bytesInDoc`: Same as `bytestIn` but only includes bytes until Document Complete event.

- `connections`: The number of connections used.

- `requests`: List of details of all requests on tested page.

- `requestsDoc`: The number of requests until Document Complete event.

- `responses_200`: The number of responses with HTTP status code of 200, OK.

- `responses_404`: The number of responses with HTTP status code of 404, not found.

- `responses_other`: The number of responses with HTTPS status code different from 200 or 404.

- `result`: Test result code. 0 (success) or 99999 (content error) are successful tests, and all other results are errors as follows:

  — 0: Successful Test

  — 4xx-5xx: HTTP Result (Base Page Error)

  — 99996: Test Failed waiting for specified DOM element/End condition

  — 99997: Test Timed Out (no content errors)

  — 99998: Test Timed Out (content errors)

  — 99999: Test Completed successfully but individual requests failed (content errors)

- `render`: The first point in time (in ms) that something was displayed to the screen. Before that user was staring at a blank page. This does not necessarily mean the user saw the page content—it could just be something as simple as a background color—but it is the first indication of something happening for the user.

- `fullyLoaded`: The time (in ms) the page took to be fully loaded—e.g., 2 seconds of no network activity after Document Complete. This will usually include any activity that is triggered by javascript after the main page loads.

- `cached`: 0 for first view or 1 for repeat view.

- `docTime`: Same as `loadTime`.

- `domTime`: The total time in ms until a given DOM element (specified via `domelement` parameter when running a test) was found on the page.

- `score_cache`: WebPageTest performance review score for leveraging browser caching of static assets.

- `score_cdn`: WebPageTest performance review score for using CDN for all static assets.

- `score_gzip`: WebPageTest performance review score for using gzip compression for transferring compressable responses.

- `score_cookies`: WebPageTest performance review score for not using cookies on static assets.

- `score_keep-alive`: WebPageTest performance review score for using persistent connections.

- `score_minify`: WebPageTest performance review score for minifying text static assets.

- `score_combine`: WebPageTest performance review score for bundling JavaScript and/or CSS assets.

- `score_compress`: WebPageTest performance review score for compressing images.

- `score_etags`: WebPageTest performance review score for disabling *ETag*s.

- `gzip_total`: Total bytes of compressible responses.

- `gzip_savings`: Total bytes of compressed responses.

- `minify_total`: Total bytes of minifiable text static assets.

- `minify_savings`: Total bytes of minified text static assets.

- `image_total`: Total bytes of images.

- `image_savings`: Total bytes of compressed images.

- `optimization_checked`: Whether or not optmizations were checked. It can be disabled with `noopt=1` parameter when running tests.

- `aft`: Above the Fold Time (no longer supported). The time taken to load everything in the viewport above the fold.

- `domElements`: The total number of DOM elements.

- `pageSpeedVersion`: The Page Speed version used on performance analysis.

- `title`: Page title.

- `titleTime`: Total time in ms until page title was set on browser.

- `loadEventStart`: Time in ms since navigation started until `window.onload` event was triggered (from W3C Navigation Timing).

- `loadEventEnd`: Time in ms since navigation started until `window.onload` event finished.

- `domContentLoadedEventStart`: Time in ms since navigation started until document `DOMContentLoaded` event was triggered (from W3C Navigation Timing).

- `domContentLoadedEventEnd`: Time in ms since navigation started until document `DOMContentLoaded` event finished.

- `lastVisualChange`: Time in ms until the last visual changed occured.

- `browser_name`: The browser name.

- `browser_version`: The browser version.

- `server_count`: Number of IP addresses that were returned in the DNS lookup for the domains.

- `server_rtt`: Estimated round-trip time to server.

- `base_page_cdn`: The CDN provider for the base page.

- `adult_site`: Flag if website (URL or title) is listed in the settings/adult.txt file.

- `fixed_viewport`: Flag if page has meta tag `viewport` set.

- `score_progressive_jpeg`: WebPageTest performance review score for using progressive JPEG.

- `firstPaint`: RUM First Paint Time, the time in ms when browser first painted something on screen. It's calculated on the client for browsers that implement this method.

- `docCPUms`: CPU busy time in ms until Document Complete event.

- `fullyLoadedCPUms`: CPU busy time in ms until page was fully loaded.

- `docCPUpct`: Average CPU utilization up until page content has loaded (`window.onload`).

- `fullyLoadedCPUpct`: Average CPU utilization up until page is fully loaded.

- `isResponsive`: Flag indicating if page is responsive. It basically checks if page body has a scrollbar in a narrow browser.

- `date`: Time and date (number of seconds since Epoch) when test was complete.

- `SpeedIndex`: The SpeedIndex score.

- `visualComplete`: Time in ms when page was visually completed.

- `run`: The run number.

- `effectiveBps`: Bytes per seconds, i.e.: total of bytes in / total time to load the page.

- `effectiveBpsDoc`: Same as `effectiveBps` but until Document Complete event.

- `tester`: The ID of tester that performed the page test.

- `userTimes`: W3C user timing marks, if any.

    — `metric1`: First metric.

    — `metricN`: Nth metric.

- `userTime.metric1`: Same as `userTimes.metric1`.

- `userTime.metricN`: Same as `userTimes.metricN`.

- custom: List of custom metrics, e.g., ["custom1", "customN"]
- custom1: First custom metric.
- customN: Nth custom metric.

Details of Requests In Test Results

requests is an array of request details and contains the following properties:

- method: The HTTP method.
- host: The host and port number of the resource being requested.
- url: The request path.
- responseCode: HTTP status code.
- load_ms: The time in ms it took the page to load.
- ttfb_ms: Time to first byte—i.e., the duration from making the request to the first byte of resource being received by the browser.
- load_start: Time elapsed in ms since test started until request actually started.
- bytesOut: The total bytes sent to request resource.
- bytesIn: The amount of data that browser had to download in order to load the requested resource.
- objectSize: The amount of encoded data resource takes.
- expires: Resource cache expiration date, the same returned in the Expires response headers.
- cacheControl: Resource cache control, the same returned in the Cache-Control response headers.
- contentType: Resource content type, the same returned in the Content-Type response headers.
- contentEncoding: Resource content encoding, the same returned in the Content-Encoding response headers.
- type: Internal use and legacy. The socket connections and DNS requests for URLBlast are written as separate entries in the data log, and those have different types. When it is processed they are discarded and only type 3 is left.
- socket: The connection ID used to download request resource.
- score_cache: WebPageTest performance review score for leveraging browser caching of requested resource.

- `score_cdn`: WebPageTest performance review score for using CDN on requested resource.
- `score_gzip`: WebPageTest performance review score for using gzip compression for transferring compressable resource responses.
- `score_cookies`: WebPageTest performance review score for not using cookies on requested resource.
- `score_keep-alive`: WebPageTest performance review score for using persistent connection on requested resource.
- `score_minify`: WebPageTest performance review score for minifying text resource.
- `score_combine`: WebPageTest performance review score for bundling JavaScript and/or CSS resources.
- `score_compress`: WebPageTest performance review score for compressing images resource.
- `score_etags`: WebPageTest performance review score for disabling *ETag*s on requested resource.
- `is_secure`: Whether or not resource is under a secure connection.
- `dns_ms`: `dns_end` minus `dns_start`.
- `connect_ms`: `connect_end` minus `connect_start`.
- `ssl_ms`: `ssl_end` minus `ssl_start`.
- `gzip_total`: Total bytes of compressible response.
- `gzip_save`: Total bytes of compressed response.
- `minify_total`: Total bytes of minifiable text response.
- `minify_save`: Total bytes of minified text response.
- `image_total`: Total bytes of image resource.
- `image_save`: Total bytes of compressed image resource.
- `cache_time`: Total cache duration in seconds.
- `cdn_provider`: The resource CDN provider.
- `dns_start`: Time elapsed in ms since test started until request DNS lookup started.
- `dns_end`: Time elapsed in ms since test started until request DNS lookup ended.
- `connect_start`: Time elapsed in ms since test started until request TCP connection handshake started.

- connect_end: Time elapsed in ms since test started until request TCP connection handshake ended.

- ssl_start: Time elapsed in ms since test started until request SSL negotiation started.

- ssl_end: Time elapsed in ms since test started until request SSL negotiation ended.

- server_count: Number of IP addresses that were returned in the DNS lookup for the resource domain.

- client_port: Socket port on the client side for the connection that the request used (useful for matching to tcpdump).

- jpeg_scan_count: The number of scans on progressive JPEG image resources.

- full_url: Full requested URL, including URI scheme.

- score_progressive_jpeg: WebPageTest performance review score for image resource using progressive JPEG.

- load_end: Time elapsed in ms since test started until response actually ended.

- ttfb_start: Time elapsed in ms since test started until resource time to first (downloaded) byte started.

- ttfb_end: Time elapsed in ms since test started until resource time to first (downloaded) byte ended.

- download_start: Time elapsed in ms since test started until resource download started.

- download_end: Time elapsed in ms since test started until resource download ended.

- download_ms: download_end minus download_start.

- all_start: Same as load_start.

- all_end: Same as load_end.

- all_ms: all_end minus all_start.

- headers:
  — request: Array of raw request headers, one per line.
  — response: Array of raw response headers, one per line.

- index: The request index.

- number: index + 1.

API

This is an exhaustive list of all WebPageTest API endpoints.

 New releases of WebPageTest may introduce API endpoint changes. Check WebPageTest releases (*https://github.com/WPO-Foundation/webpagetest/releases*) for more details.

Locations

List of locations and the number of pending tests:

Endpoint
    /getLocations.php

Parameters

    f=*format*
        The output format:

            • json
            • xml (default)

    callback=*name*
        When used in conjunction with f=json, returns JSONP—i.e., wraps the JSON output with given callback function name.

    r=*request id>*
        Echoes a given request ID. Useful for tracking asynchronous requests.

Output
    • XML by default or if f=xml is present
    • JSON if f=json is present
    • JSONP if f=json and callback=*name* are present

Test

Submit a URL or script to be tested, returning a test ID and other information about the submitted test:

Endpoint
    /runtest.php

Parameters

url=*url*
> The URL to be tested. Must be encoded in order to escape URI-specific characters.

k=*api key*
> The WebPageTest API key if required by server.

location=*location*
> Location to test from.

connectivity=*profile*
> Connectivity profile:
>
> - Cable (default)
> - DSL
> - FIOS
> - Dial
> - 3G
> - 3GFast
> - Native
> - Custom, if connectivity=custom then location=*location*, bwDown=*bandwidth* and bwUp=*bandwidth* are required and optionally latency=*time* and plr=*percentage*.

runs=*number*
> Number of test runs; defaults to 1.

fvonly=1
> Skip the repeat-view test.

video=1
> Capture video.

private=1
> Keep the test hidden from the test log.

label=*label*
> Label for the test.

web10=1
> Stop test at document complete. Typically, tests run until all activity stops.

`noscript=1`
> Disable JavaScript.

`clearcerts=1`
> Clear SSL certificate caches.

`ignoreSSL=1`
> Ignore SSL certificate errors—e.g., name mismatch, self-signed certificates, etc.

`standards=1`
> Forces all pages to load in standard mode (IE only).

`tcpdump=1`
> Capture network packet trace (`tcpdump`).

`bodies=1`
> Save response bodies for text resources.

`keepua=1`
> Do not add `PTST` to the original browser user agent string.

`domelement=element`
> `DOM element` to record for submeasurement.

`time=seconds`
> Minimum test duration in seconds.

`tester=name`
> Run the test on a specific PC (name must match exactly or the test will not run).

`mobile=1`
> Emulate mobile browser (experimental): Chrome mobile user agent, 640x960 screen, 2x scaling, and fixed viewport (Chrome only).

`timeline=1`
> Capture Developer Tools Timeline (Chrome only).

`timelineStack=1`
> Set between 1 and 5 to include the JavaScript call stack. Must be used in conjunction with timeline (increases overhead; Chrome only).

`trace=1`
> Capture chrome trace (about://tracing; Chrome only).

`netlog=1`
> Capture Network Log (Chrome only).

`dataReduction=1`
Enable `data reduction` on Chrome 34+ Android (Chrome only).

`uastring=`*string*
Custom user agent string (Chrome only).

`cmdline=`*switches*
Use a list of custom command-line switches (Chrome only).

`username=`*username*
Username for authenticating tests (HTTP authentication).

`password=`*password*
Password for authenticating tests (HTTP authentication).

`sensitive=1`
Discard script and HTTP headers in the result.

`noheaders=1`
Disable saving of the HTTP headers, as well as browser status messages and CPU utilization.

`block=`*urls*
Space-delimited list of URLs to block (substring match).

`spof=`*domains*
Space-delimited list of domains to simulate failure by rerouting to *black-hole.webpagetest.org* to silently drop all requests.

`custom=`*script*
Execute arbitrary JavaScript at the end of a test to collect custom metrics.

`authType=`*type*
Type of authentication:

- `0: Basic` (default)
- `1: SNS`

`notify=`*email*
Email address to notify with the test results.

`pingback=`*url*
URL to ping when the test is complete (the test ID will be passed as an `id` parameter).

bwDown=*bandwidth*
> Download bandwidth in Kbps (used when specifying a custom connectivity profile).

bwUp=*bandwidth*
> Upload bandwidth in Kbps (used when specifying a custom connectivity profile).

latency=*time*
> First-hop round-trip time in ms (used when specifying a custom connectivity profile).

plr=*percentage*
> Packet loss rate, which is the percent of packets to drop (used when specifying a custom connectivity profile).

noopt=1
> Disable optimization checks (for faster testing).

noimages=1
> Disable screenshot capturing.

pngss=1
> Save a full-resolution version of the fully loaded screenshot as a PNG.

iq=*level*
> JPEG compression level (30–100) for the screenshots and video capture.

mv=1
> Store the video from the median run when capturing video is enabled.

htmlbody=1
> Save the content of only the base HTML response.

tsview_id=*id*
> Test name to use when submitting results to tsviewdb (for private instances that have integrated with tsviewdb).

affinity=*string*
> String to hash test to a specific test agent. Tester will be picked by index among available testers.

blockads=1
> Block ads defined by *adblockrules.org*.

continuousVideo=1
> Capture video continuously (unstable/experimental; may cause tests to fail).

```
forceSpdy3=1
```
Force SPDY version 3 (Chrome only).

```
swrender=1
```
Force software rendering; disable GPU acceleration (Chrome only).

```
r=request id
```
Echoes a given request ID. Useful for tracking asynchronous requests.

Output
- JSON or XML if `f=format` is present
- JSONP if `f=json` and `callback=name` are present

Status

Check the current status of the submitted test:

Endpoint
```
/testStatus.php
```

Parameters

```
test=test id
```
The submitted test ID.

```
f=format
```
The output format:

- `json` (default)
- `xml`

```
callback=name
```
When used in conjunction with `f=json` (default), returns JSONP—i.e., wraps the JSON output with given callback function name.

```
r=request id
```
Echoes a given request ID. Useful for tracking asynchronous requests.

Output
- JSON by default or if `f=json` is present
- XML if `f=xml` is present
- JSONP if `callback=name` is present with `f=format` omitted or `f=json` is present

Cancel

Cancel a running or pending test:

Endpoint
/cancelTest.php

Parameters

> test=*test id*
> > The submitted test ID.

> k=*api key*
> > The WebPageTest API key if required by server.

Output
HTML

Results

Get the test results:

Endpoint
/jsonResult.php or /xmlResult.php

Parameters

> test=*test id*
> > The submitted test ID.

> breakdown=1
> > Include the breakdown of requests and bytes by mime type.

> domains=1
> > Include the breakdown of requests and bytes by domain.

> pagespeed=1
> > Include the PageSpeed score in the response (may be slower).

> requests=1
> > Include the request data in the response (slower and results in much larger responses).

> r=*request id*
> > Echoes a given request ID. Useful for tracking asynchronous requests.

> callback=*name*
> > When used with /jsonResult.php, returns JSONP—i.e., wraps the JSON output with given callback function name.

Output

- JSON when using `/jsonResult.php`

- JSONP when using `/jsonResult.php` with `callback=name`

- XML when using `/xmlResult.php`

Testers

List tester's status and details:

Endpoint

`/getTesters.php`

Parameters

`f=format`
The output format:

- `xml` (default)

- `json`

`callback=name`
When used in conjunction with `f=json`, returns JSONP—i.e., wraps the JSON output with given `callback` function name.

`r=request id`
Echoes a given request ID. Useful for tracking asynchronous requests.

Output

- XML by default or if `f=xml` is present

- JSON if `f=json` is present

- JSONP if `f=json` and `callback=name` are present

HAR

Get the HTTP archive (HAR) from test:

Endpoint

`/export.php`

Parameters

`test=test id`
The completed test ID.

callback=*name*
> Returns JSONP—i.e., wraps the JSON output with given callback function name.

Output
- JSON
- JSONP when callback=*name* is present

Chrome Developer Tools Timeline

Get the Chrome Developer Tools Timeline data (if available) from test:

Endpoint
> /getTimeline.php

Parameters

test=*test id*
> The completed test ID.

run=*number*
> Run number on a multiple runs test; defaults to 1 (first run).

cached=1
> Get the repeat view (cached view) instead of default first view (primed cache).

Output
> JSON

Test History

Get history of previously run tests:

Endpoint
> /testLog.php

Parameters

f=csv
> Output data as CSV; if omitted, HTML page is returned.

days=*number*
> Get history for last *number* days, including the current day.

from=*date*
> Initial date in the format YYYY-MM-DD. It queries backwards, starting from *date* going back to *number* of days in the past.

filter=*string*
> Narrow search for tests with URLs containing *string*.

video=1
> Narrow search for tests that include video.

all=1
> Search for tests from all users.

nolimit=1
> Do not limit number of results (100 by default). Warning: might be slow.

Output
> CSV; f=csv must be present

Response Body

Get response body for text resources from test if response bodies parameter was set on submitted test.

Endpoint
> /response_body.php

Parameters

test=*test id*
> The completed test ID.

request=*number*
> The request number; defaults to 1 which is the HTML document.

run=*number*
> Run number on a multiple runs test; defaults to 1 (first run).

cached=1
> Get the repeat view (cached view) instead of default first view (primed cache).

Output
> text/plain

Waterfall

Get the waterfall PNG image:

Endpoint
    /waterfall.php

Parameters

    test=*test id*
        The completed test ID.

    run=*number*
        Run number on a multiple runs test; defaults to 1 (first run).

    cached=1
        Get the repeat view (cached view) instead of default first view (primed cache).

    type=*chart*
        Chart type: waterfall (default) or connection.

    mime=1
        Chart coloring by MIME type.

    width=*px*
        Chart image width in pixels between 300 and 2000; defaults to 930.

    max=*seconds*
        Maximum time in seconds; defaults to automatic.

    requests=*items*
        Filter requests (e.g., 1,2,3,4-9,8); defaults to all.

    cpu=0
        Hide CPU utilization.

    bw=0
        Hide bandwidth utilization.

    dots=0
        Hide ellipsis (…) for missing items.

    labels=0
        Hide labels for requests.

Output
    image/png (binary)

Create Video

Create a video for single or multiple tests:

Endpoint
    /video/create.php

Parameters

tests=*test ids*
    One or more comma separated test ID.

end=*end point*
    Frame comparison end point:

- visual: visually complete (default)
- all: last change
- doc: document complete
- full: fully loaded

f=*format*
    The output format (required; otherwise, it redirects to video view page):

- json
- xml

callback=*name*
    When used in conjunction with f=json, returns JSONP—i.e., wraps the JSON output with given callback function name.

Output
- JSON or XML if f=*format* is present
- JSONP if f=json and callback=*name* are present

Get Gzip Content

Get several test data stored in WebPageTest server:

Endpoint
    /getgzip.php

Parameters

test=*test id*
    The completed test ID.

file=*filename*
    Get data of one of the following files:

- testinfo.json

    Get test details.

- <run>_[Cached_]pagespeed.txt

    Get the Google Page Speed JSON results (if available) from test.

- <run>_[Cached_]progress.csv

    Get the CPU, bandwidth, and memory utilization CSV data from test.

- <run>_[Cached_]IEWTR.txt

    Get the request TSV data from test.

- <run>_[Cached_]netlog.txt

    Get the Chrome Developer Tools Net log JSON data (if available) from test.

- <run>_[Cached_]trace.json

    Get the Chrome Trace JSON data (if available) from test.

- <run>_[Cached_]console_log.json

    Get the browser console log JSON data (if available) from test.

    Where:

    — run: run number.

    — Cached_: if provided, get repeat view.

- <run>_[Cached_]screen[_render|_doc].<jpg|png>

    Get the fully loaded page screenshot, where:

    — _render: if provided, get the page screenshot at the Start Render point (i.e., when something was first displayed on screen).

    — _doc: if provided, get the page screenshot at the Document Complete point (i.e., when window.onload was fired).

    — jpg: get screenshot in JPG format.

    — png: get screenshot in PNG in full resolution if test was submitted with pngss=1.

Get Thumbnail

Get thumbnail for screenshot and waterfall:

Endpoint
    /thumbnail.php

Parameters

test=*test id*
    The completed test ID.

file=*filename*
    One of the following files:

* <run>_[Cached_]screen[_render|_doc].<jpg|png>

    Get the fully loaded page screenshot thumbnail, where:

    — run: run number.

    — Cached_: if provided, get repeat view screenshot thumbnail.

    — _render: if provided, get the page screenshot thumbnail at the Start Render point (i.e., when something was first displayed on screen).

* _doc: if provided, get the page screenshot thumbnail at the Document Complete point (i.e., when window.onload was fired).

    — jpg: get screenshot thumbnail in JPG format.

    — png: get screenshot thumbnail in PNG if in full resolution.

* <run>_[Cached_]waterfall.png

    Get the test run waterfall thumbnail, where:

    — run: run number.

    — Cached_: if provided, get repeat view waterfall thumbnail

        Thumbnail waterfall has optional parameters:

    — type=*chart*

        Chart type: waterfall (default) or connection.

    — mime=1

        Chart coloring by MIME type.

    — width=*px*

        Chart image width in pixels between 300 and 2000; defaults to 930.

    — max=*seconds*

Maximum time in seconds; defaults to automatic.

— `requests=`*items*

Filter requests (e.g., 1,2,3,4–9,8); defaults to all.

— `cpu=0`

Hide CPU utilization.

— `bw=0`

Hide bandwidth utilization.

— `dots=0`

Hide ellipsis (…) for missing items.

— `labels=0`

Hide labels for requests.

Index

A
age of resources, 34-35
Amazon Machine Images (AMI), 133-136
Amazon S3 Storage, 158
Amazon Web Services (AWS), 133-136
Android test device, 144-147
antipatterns, 19-24, 51
    canceled requests, 21-23
    long first-byte time, 19-20
    network silence, 23-24
    reopened connections, 20-21
Apache, 136
API key
    limitations, 102
    specifying, 115
application-specific metrics, 2
archiving tests, 157-158
assertion comparisons, 122
assertion test specs file, 121
authentication, 84-87
    DOM manipulation, 86
    HTTP Basic Authentication (HBA), 84
    setting cookies, 86-87

B
bandwidth, 65, 151
base tag, 22
black hole rerouting, 91-96
    setDns command, 92-93
    SPOF tab, 94-96
blackhole.webpagetest.org, 93
block command, 97
blog pages, 60
browsers, breakdown by, 62-64

C
caches/caching
    analyzing cachability, 34-35
    cache optimization, 31-37
    cache states, 81
    caching static content, 28
    defined, 31
    heuristic caching, 35-37
    overview, 31-32
    Repeat View, 32-34
canceled requests, 21
Capture Video, 40-41
Chrome
    desktop emulation in, 74
    emulation mode, 77-78
    testing by processing breakdown, 126
compress transfer, 27
connection speed, 68-72
connection view, 17-18, 51
connections, reusing, 20-21, 25, 26
content delivery networks (CDNs), 25, 28
content download, 12, 18
continuous integration (CI), 113-129
    asserting metrics from test results, 120-126
        (see also test specs)
    Jenkins integration, 126-127
    Node.js wrapper, 113-120
        (see also Node.js wrapper)
    Travis-CI, 127-129
cookies, setting, 86-87
critical path, 17

D
data table, 8-9

X

/xmlResult.php, 109, 111

Y

Yahoo!, 24

YouTube, 2

YSlow, 24

About the Authors

Rick Viscomi is a frontend engineer and web performance evangelist. He has leveraged the power of WebPageTest to help speed up the websites of the Travel Channel, Food Network, and HGTV. Since 2013, he has worked at Google to make YouTube fast.

Andy Davies first stumbled into web performance in late 1990s, when he was trying to deliver elearning over dial-up connection speeds, and has been hooked ever since. He's currently associate director for web performance at NCC Group, where he helps clients measure and improve the performance of their websites. Andy regularly speaks about web performance and occasionally contributes to open source projects such as WebPageTest. He also wrote *A Pocket Guide to Web Performance* (Five Simple Steps).

Marcel Duran is a web performance engineer at Google. He previously worked to speed up high-traffic websites for Twitter and Yahoo! He was also the frontend lead for Yahoo!'s Exceptional Performance Team, where he open sourced YSlow. Marcel also spoke at the Velocity Conference and coauthored *Web Performance Daybook Volume 2* (O'Reilly).

Colophon

The animal on the cover of *Using WebPageTest* is a *large-spotted genet (Genetta tigrina)*. It is also known as a cape genet or blotched genet. They are native to South Africa and other areas of southern Africa. They live near lakes, rivers, and other bodies of water with sufficient tree coverage.

Adult large-spotted genets can weigh between 2 and 8 pounds. Their bodies will grow in length between 19 and 23 inches, while the tail will be between 16 and 22 inches. Females are slightly smaller in size than males. They are larger than their common (or small-spotted) genet relatives and have different coloring, which helps distinguish between the two subspecies.

The large-spotted genet has a dark dorsal stripe along the length of its back. The base color of its fur is of light brown/gray color. The irregular spots and stripes among its fur are a dark brown. In small-spotted or common genets, the stripes of the tail are lighter in color. The large-spotted genet is similar to a cat in numerous ways: they hiss, have semiretractable claws, and are quite independent, among other things.

This animal is solitary, nocturnal, and carnivorous. They hunt at night with a diet that consists of rodents, birds, and insects. Though compared to cats and ferrets in terms of behavior and hunting methods, it is discouraged to get a genet as an exotic household pet as they tend to shun affection and companionship as they grow older.

Many of the animals on O'Reilly covers are endangered; all of them are important to the world. To learn more about how you can help, go to *animals.oreilly.com*.

The cover image is from *Wood's Animate Creation*. The cover fonts are URW Typewriter and Guardian Sans. The text font is Adobe Minion Pro; the heading font is Adobe Myriad Condensed; and the code font is Dalton Maag's Ubuntu Mono.

Get even more for your money.

Join the O'Reilly Community, and register the O'Reilly books you own. It's free, and you'll get:

- $4.99 ebook upgrade offer
- 40% upgrade offer on O'Reilly print books
- Membership discounts on books and events
- Free lifetime updates to ebooks and videos
- Multiple ebook formats, DRM FREE
- Participation in the O'Reilly community
- Newsletters
- Account management
- 100% Satisfaction Guarantee

Signing up is easy:

1. Go to: oreilly.com/go/register
2. Create an O'Reilly login.
3. Provide your address.
4. Register your books.

Note: English-language books only

To order books online:
oreilly.com/store

For questions about products or an order:
orders@oreilly.com

To sign up to get topic-specific email announcements and/or news about upcoming books, conferences, special offers, and new technologies:
elists@oreilly.com

For technical questions about book content:
booktech@oreilly.com

To submit new book proposals to our editors:
proposals@oreilly.com

O'Reilly books are available in multiple DRM-free ebook formats. For more information:
oreilly.com/ebooks

Have it your way.